Ground Games
—————— for Horses

WALTRAUD BÖHMKE

Ground Games
—————— for Horses

SKILLS, TESTS, OBSTACLES, AND
26 ENGAGING IN-HAND COURSES

TRAFALGAR SQUARE
North Pomfret. Vermont

Disclaimer of Liability
The author and publisher shall have neither liability nor responsibility to any person or entity with respect to any loss or damage caused or alleged to be caused directly or indirectly by the information contained in this book. While the book is as accurate as the author can make it, there may be errors, omissions, and inaccuracies.

Trafalgar Square Books encourages the use of approved riding helmets in all equestrian sports and activities.

Trafalgar Square Books certifies that the content in this book was generated by a human expert on the subject, and the content was edited, fact-checked, and proofread by human publishing specialists with a lifetime of equestrian knowledge. TSB does not publish books generated by artificial intelligence (AI).

ISBN: 978-1-64601-223-7
Library of Congress Control Number: 2024937450

Photography: Gudrun Braun/KOSMOS (pp vi, vii, 4, 5, 10, 11, 22, 28, 30, 31, 32, 33, 34, 37, 51, 52, 53, 54 top, 55, 56, 57, 58 bottom, 65, 66 left, 73, 74, 81, 82), Christiane Slawik/KOSMOS (page 19), Inge Vogel (pp 66 right, 67, 68), Pauline von Hardenberg/KOSMOS (pp viii, 1, 2, 3, 6, 7, 8, 9, 12, 13, 14, 15, 17, 18, 23, 24, 25, 26, 27, 43, 45, 52 upper right, 54 bottom, 58 top, 63, 83)
Illustrations: Cornelia Koller/KOSMOS
Cover design: RM Didier
German editor: Gudrun Braun
Interior design concept: Peter Schmidt Group GmbH, Hamburg
Interior design: W. Kohlhammer Druckerei GmbH + Co. KG
Production: Claudia Frank
Translation into English: Karin Nifong

Printed in the United States of America
10 9 8 7 6 5 4 3 2 1

☞ Table of Contents

GROUNDWORK IS TEAMWORK

The first contact between human and horse usually happens on the ground, in-hand. Even if you intend to ride or drive the horse, you'll first have to retrieve the horse from the stall, paddock, or pasture—in-hand.

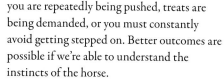

To this end, it's worth it to have a solid understanding of equine habits and behaviors. It's during our daily handling of the horse—when we are leading, cleaning, bridling, and tacking—that we establish the foundation for trusting and safe interaction. The 26 sample lessons in this book are meant to develop the horse into a well-mannered partner, through systematic training. This makes relaxed teamwork possible. It's more difficult to build a positive emotional relationship with a horse if

you are repeatedly being pushed, treats are being demanded, or you must constantly avoid getting stepped on. Better outcomes are possible if we're able to understand the instincts of the horse.

The horse lives as a herd animal within a group of his own species, in a functional social structure. As a human, you are ostensibly the weaker partner, at least when it comes to your physical power and strength. Therefore, you should try to gain as much knowledge about equine habitats and "language" as possible.

When you learn how horses communicate with each other, you're able to prepare for and then interact with the horse in a calm, fair manner. The handler must respect and acknowledge the individual space of the horse, and then communicate to the horse that the handler, as the higher-ranking member of this "interactive horse group team," wants to be equally respected and acknowledged. Clear rules give horses a sense of safety within their human-designed environments.

Therefore, the goal should be to establish a good, respectful, harmonious interaction between human and horse where both parties feel comfortable with each other, trust each other, and can count on each other.

GROUNDWORK EXERCISES

Training begins with simple exercises, and depends on the horse's level of knowledge, not just the knowledge and abilities of the handler. Start with individual tasks or obstacles before combining them into a series of exercises that offer meaningful progression. This way, you revisit and reinforce newly learned skills.

Sequences of distinct, clearly defined exercises offer the opportunity to compare yourself and your horse to other participants, and receive feedback and suggestions for further training based on that comparison.

Predetermined routes and exercises challenge you as the handler to be exact in the coordination of your aids in order to guide the horse through performing the tasks with precision. Reaching these small goals promotes mutual trust and creates reliability and certainty even during unfamiliar exercises—or out on the trail. Positive experiences and the knowledge that the horse will listen when aids are applied in a correct, precise, and timely manner offer self-confidence to the handler and create a clear framework for the horse.

The appropriate training load depends on the age of the horse and his physical and mental condition. Young horses tire as quickly as small children do, and can only be taught in short training increments (5 to 15 minutes). Adult horses with more mental capacity can manage slightly longer sessions—up to 30 minutes. Short breaks within training sessions help improve the horse's ability to focus, and successful completion of exercises gives the horse a sense of confidence and satisfaction.

INTRODUCTION TO GROUNDWORK
Varied Training with the Horse

TRUST AND FUN WITH GROUNDWORK

Everyone who wants to interact with horses should learn about the needs and behavior of equines. Only then can you handle these lovable animals in a horse-appropriate way and have a joyful relationship with them.

FOUNDATIONS FOR TRUST

Horses are able to mirror their human partners precisely. They want to accommodate and trust them. Exercises in groundwork offer a very solid base to that end, and can be applied to riding or driving, too. However, applying these training efforts to multiple areas does require certain skills, which I will discuss in the following pages.

"Groundwork" is interaction with the horse from the ground. It lays the foundation for harmonious interaction between human and horse. Teaching the horse good ground manners creates a basis for a trusting and respectful partnership in all areas of equestrian sports. It also serves to ensure the safety of both human and equine.

— The training of the horse must be organized and built upon sensibly and in small increments in order to suit horse and human equally.

— It must systematically progress from initially easy exercises to more difficult ones.

Going through a pole cross with trust and confidence.

A confident team even in open terrain.

One of the horse's ears is turned toward the handler ...

— Every exercise has a series of drills that must be applied correctly.

— The horse must go through training sessions regularly to encourage continuous progress.

— The training must be varied and well rounded.

— The horse's motivation must be sparked and then maintained.

— Physical and mental overload must be avoided.

The goal of groundwork with the horse should always be a trusting, harmonious interaction with the horse, regardless of his breed, age, and occupation. Groundwork that is done well is fun for both the human and the horse.

HUMAN AND HORSE

During this training, the handler must orient herself within the structure of a horse herd. The horse needs her to show confidence and leadership. Self-assured horses who have a higher rank within their group need to be handled differently than those who are lower-ranking, anxious, or timid.

"Higher-ranking" does not automatically mean that these horses are "sassy" or "do not want to cooperate." If they have a very friendly personality and display efficient self-assurance in their surroundings, they can be great partners for insecure or anxious handlers.

By contrast, lower-ranking horses may try to seize the opportunity to finally hold a leadership position, and may be more likely to question requests from their handlers. Clear

... which is a sign of a trusting relationship.

requests from the handler need to channel this kind of behavior in the right direction. That requires experience and self-confidence from the handler. An insecure demeanor will result in unnecessary "discussions."

The same applies to anxious horses. They require leadership that is assertive and built on trust and expertise. The more naturally a handler can achieve this demeanor, the more willingly the horse will follow her directions. But inconsiderate or overly dominant behavior from the handler will lead to problems, as the horse will want to get away from this stressful situation. He'll react either hesitantly or hastily to the requests of his handler, and he'll want to escape if he has the chance.

COMMUNICATION

Communication between humans happens predominantly through verbal language; horses, on the other hand, communicate with each other mostly through body language. This means humans must learn to use body language effectively in order to be able to communicate with the horse.

If a handler is feeling uncertain, that's revealed through body language just as easily as tension and learned dominant behavior. Horses will reflect the feeling the handler is bringing into their personal space with hesitation and defensive actions.

Misinterpretations of the horse's reactions by us, their human counterparts, might lead

This girl is wearing a riding helmet, riding gloves, and ankle-high boots.

to unintended conflicts that often only become noticeable over time. Therefore, we must act in a clear and unambiguous manner. The cues the handler gives the horse with the movement of her body, her voice, and her aids through the lead rope, reins, and other tools should always have the same meaning.

The intensity of a request should always start at the minimum. Only after the horse doesn't respond appropriately should that intensity be raised—in small increments—until the horse gives the desired reaction. This is the only way you can get an attentive, willing, and motivated horse who will cooperate readily and execute all tasks happily and with ease, and who can be relied on in unfamiliar and new situations because he has learned how to trust.

This trusting relationship must be carefully fostered and maintained. Horses like to know who looks out for whom and who protects whom. They experience this and decide this amongst themselves with small and—to human eyes—often inconspicuous rituals, although there can be obvious signals as well. A handler must recognize when the horse is "checking" her leadership like this and respond with confidence. That means she should handle the horse assuredly and without fear.

It's not usually necessary to employ dominant behavior to ensure that the horse accepts his handler as a leader. Horses don't constantly push each other away or punish each other; they prefer to respect each other, and are capable of creating tight and long-lasting friendships, too.

Horses want to have reliable partnerships that make them feel secure and protected. During everyday situations, a horse will willingly follow the requests of his handler, whether he is being taken from his stall, fetched from the pasture, tacked up, cared for by a farrier, loading into a trailer, and so on. This collaboration of human and horse is subject to clear rules. But the horse as an individual shouldn't be a puppet. He should be trained with an eye toward his abilities and

Teamwork in perfect balance.

EQUIPMENT FOR HUMAN AND HORSE

Equipment for the handler during ground-work includes sturdy, ankle-high boots, long pants, gloves, and a shirt that covers her torso and shoulders. When handling difficult horses, you should wear a helmet, too. For the horse, you can usually use a rope halter with a lead rope, which allows for supple handling and guidance. Highly trained or sensitive horses might be better off in a well-fitted leather or nylon halter. Using a bridle is another option, in combination with a whip as a forward driving aid.

As you continue to work through the exercises toward improvement of the horse's flexion and bend, a bridle or cavesson is useful.

In exceptional cases—when a horse isn't willing to cooperate in a rope halter, or perhaps when handling stallions—a chain may be used temporarily, by experienced handlers, to correct the horse. A chain may only be used in combination with a leather or nylon halter.

To put a chain on correctly, thread the snap hook from the left side through the left ring of the halter. It should then go from

disposition—what he's good at, and what he enjoys. The handler has to achieve a certain level of proficiency, with in-depth knowledge and experience that allow her to interpret equine behavior correctly and react accordingly.

A beaming face says a thousand words—this is a loving relationship.

This pinto mare spots her own shadow on the tarp and spooks suddenly, pushing into her handler's space.

In this kind of situation, it's important to stay calm and not lose control.

bottom to top, and from outside to inside, around the nosepiece of the halter. Then, thread it through the ring on the right side and buckle it to the upper ring on the right side of the horse's head (where the crownpiece starts). Do *not* jerk on or pull the chain. That can result in extreme defensive reactions, especially when handling sensitive horses. Never pull the chain through the mouth, and *never* tie horses with the chain—either one risks serious injury.

CHANGE OF DIRECTION

After a change of direction, you may notice the horse experiencing the same object differently from this new viewpoint, and shying away or hesitating all over again. You should give the horse time to explore as if the

situation is brand new. The more closely the horse can inspect new objects or situations, the sooner he'll walk past them without hesitation, in either direction.

OBTRUSIVENESS AND PERSONAL SPACE

Every living creature establishes personal space and distance from others. Anyone who crosses into this personal space causes a reaction.

Typically, with horses the higher-ranking individual defends his space, and the lower-ranking one must back away—and, in doing so, grants more personal space to his higher-ranking fellow horse.

With horses who are friends, or who are grooming each other, the higher-ranking

Repeating the exercise safely and with clear focus—but with noticeable tension lingering on the handler's side.

horse might allow a decrease in the range of his personal space, but he will also decide the length of time this reduction lasts.

In moments of uncertainty or fear, most living creatures move closer together to appear more compact and powerful.

However, in the context of this groundwork training, if a horse doesn't respect his handler's personal space during their interaction, she may be injured (if he steps on her foot, if she trips, if he nips her, and so on).

Therefore, the handler must establish a set distance between herself and the horse, and that distance must be respected by both of them. Petting and scratching the horse is allowed, of course, preferably on body parts like the crest, withers, or back, as a way of praising him and strengthening the relationship and connection. Here, the handler chooses the duration and intensity of the petting or scratching.

RESISTANCE

Even during groundwork, horses can show obvious signs of resistance. Those signs might be pinned ears, a tight muzzle, threats to snap or bite, lifting a hind leg, or swishing the tail. They all need to be noted.

In these instances, the handler must act as the higher-ranking team member to prevent an escalation. At the same time, however, she needs to determine the reason for the behavior. Is the exercise too difficult and asking too much of the horse? Has she been letting the training session run too long? Are the cues not clear enough? Is the tack uncomfortable? Are there health problems?

VISUAL CUES

Visual cues include body language, the direction of the gaze, head movement, movement of the hands and arms, the direction of travel, the energy of the walk (slow and sluggish, or energetic, or rushed), breathing frequency, relaxed or nervous body tension, and perspiration.

These are all indicators the horse can use to gauge his handler's state of mind. Horses can most likely detect when a person is afraid, both with their sense of smell and by reading the person's body language. Uncertainty in someone who is supposed to be in the leader role unsettles the horse. Any doubts the horse may have had are confirmed, and he will show obvious signs of insecurity.

Insecurity can also result if the horse is flooded with too much information, through frantic, exaggerated body language or uncontrolled movement of body parts, and is expressed by ignoring the handler's requests or by rushing in his responses.

TACTILE CUES

Tactile input is a helpful way of communicating to the horse which instructions he is supposed to follow and how. Horses have a very pronounced sense of touch, which is something that should be factored in when you apply aids, by always starting out with the least amount of pressure possible. A lack of immediate response doesn't automatically mean the horse is uncooperative, but rather, more often than not, the horse did not understand the question. In that case, the aids should be repeated with greater clarity and focus.

The horse follows the handler through a tight chute of poles.

Guiding the horse through the cones with the lead rope while standing at a distance is a difficult exercise.

Sensible horses will turn into anxious horses if the tactile input of the repeated aid is too strong. They develop an urge to move without trying to understand what is asked of them. Horses might also have become desensitized to the aids. Unfortunately, desensitization happens more frequently with mild-tempered horses. This doesn't mean they don't feel the first, more softly applied aid. Horses become numb to the aids if they are applied in a constant and monotonous way, and this desensitization comes at the expense of the horse, because he will tolerate increasingly strong tactile cues without responding. To achieve quicker responses to the aids from sluggish horses, a systematic increase in the intensity of the aids is required.

For example, a normal forward driving aid is given. If there is no response, the intensity of the aid will be increased. Eventually, if a response still doesn't come, the aid will be noticeably intensified for a short moment. As soon as the horse responds, the driving aid goes away, and the horse is praised. The next application of aids should start back at a normal intensity level.

AUDITORY CUES

Vocalizations like neighing, nickering, squealing, and snorting play a minor role in communication with horses, but may still be important.

Horses recognize each other by their neighing, and can locate each other by it when they are out of each other's line of sight. Nickering is used for a relaxed, very friendly greeting at short distances.

Squealing is usually heard during fights for dominance and during mating behavior. You should be aware that squealing can sometimes be accompanied by striking with the front leg. A soft or distinct groan is usually a sign of pain in the horse.

Horses are able to perceive tone and color in human voices. Horses can also learn individual words and respond to them as cues, but the "first stop" for a horse will always be body language.

To motivate horses to step out energetically, use high-pitched, short, concise vocal cues, with smacking or kissing sounds matching the rhythm of the gait.

To reassure the horse, slow down the tempo, or perform downward transitions, use a soothing, deep, drawn-out tone. As with tactile cues, the voice should not be used constantly. Vocal cues should come when they are needed, for as short a duration as possible, until the desired response is achieved.

Lateral yielding of the hindquarters.

Point the whip towards the hind end

COMBINING CUES

The nature and extent of the aids applied depend on the desired goal and execution by the horse. Initially, the horse's attention should always be drawn by applying an auditory cue, to prepare him for the task ahead. This is followed by body language and tactile cues, applied either through the halter or a forward driving touch with lead-line or whip.

As soon as the horse responds correctly to a request, the aids are noticeably reduced or go away completely, and are only reapplied when needed.

You always start with minimal aids, which will be intensified by two to three shades if necessary. The added intensity should be applied in a way that makes sense to the horse and allows him to respond successfully. The aids shouldn't be applied continuously at the same pressure, as that will lead to desensitizing (numbing) the horse, but they also cannot be so strong that the horse will be surprised or startled, and they can't come with no warning. The aids have been applied correctly when it doesn't take long for the horse to perform the requested task willingly and calmly.

BODY LANGUAGE

Humans send a wide range of signals to the horse with their body language. Body language is the interplay of posture, movement, the direction of the gaze, and gestures, in combination with facial expressions. People are often not aware of these nonverbal cues and tend to give them unknowingly.

During groundwork, a person must learn to use these cues deliberately. That's the only way you'll be able to apply your aids in a manner precise enough for the horse to understand your request and respond willingly. People should not underestimate the fact that their moods can be easily detected by the horse. Tone of voice and body language are strongly influenced by stress, unhappiness, restlessness, anger, agitation, and fear. Naturally, these emotions can be mirrored by the horse, with obvious tension or insecurity in response to the aids, and this often results in poor performance of the task at hand.

Therefore, it is essential that humans learn to practice self-awareness and self-reflection. When handling a horse, you must remain calm and mentally balanced, and

and the horse steps sideways. *Fine-tuning: lateral movement of the hindquarters with minimal aids.*

must act controlled and level-headed, even in stressful situations.

POSTURE

— During groundwork, the handler should walk naturally upright and with light tension through the body. A deliberately straight, tense posture is as bad as a lax, sluggish one.

— The handler's head should be carried upright, with the eyes forward.

— The handler's shoulders should be set parallel to the direction of travel.

— Most of the time, the handler's body should be positioned at a right angle to the horse.

— The horse should always maintain a distance of about half an arm's length from the handler.

— The handler should walk naturally, with self-confidence, and give a competent, self-assured impression to which the horse is drawn and which the horse follows respectfully and trustingly.

MOVEMENT

— The handler's movements should be smooth and uniform, neither hesitant nor faltering.

— The handler's pace should clearly match the rhythm of the horse's gait.

— There shouldn't be any rushing in the movement of the handler's arms or legs.

— Especially while the handler is walking, her arms need to be kept still; otherwise, they become driving aids.

— The handler's overall appearance to horse and observers alike should radiate self-assuredness and confidence in handling equines.

THE DIRECTION OF THE GAZE

The handler's eyes should be looking ahead in the direction of travel, not at the ground.

— Even on bending lines or over obstacles, always look where you want to go.

— Try to avoid looking directly at the horse; this, especially in tense situations, can make the horse feel threatened. Only in relaxed situations do horses appreciate direct eye contact.

GESTURES

— The handler should avoid unintentional movement of the arms and hands; it unsettles the horse.

— The handler's leading hand should be relaxed and slightly open. Closing it into a fist gives the horse an impression of tension.

— The guidance of the lead rope or the whip should always be applied in a controlled manner and slowly increase in intensity. The horse must be able to understand the application of the aids. The aids should not suddenly startle the horse. The aids should always be given with a soft pressure at first.

— The handler should only apply specific cues, not create continuous noise.

— The handler should always apply touch precisely—in front of the shoulder joint, on the shoulder, on the back, or on the hindquarters, but never around the head.

— The handler should move only as much as she needs to in order to act clearly and consistently, with the necessary inner calm.

SAFETY CONSIDERATIONS

To ensure that groundwork with the horse is fun and doesn't result in accidents, it's

The horse can tell which direction he's supposed to go based on his handler's body language.

Guiding the horse from a distance can sometimes simplify an exercise. Here, the handler's right arm is holding the end of the lead rope and is acting as a driving aid.

important to include some considerations for safety when you plan your training sessions.

— The human-horse combination must be a good match.

— Inexperienced people should be matched with experienced, calm, safe horses.

— Both horse and human must have properly fitted and functional gear.

— Possible disturbances must be predictable (spectators, cars, tractor).

— Consider herd instincts (including separation anxiety).

— During pole work, poles must be secured so they can't roll.

— Build trust slowly—start with a few single poles.

— Set "chutes" (one pole to either side) wide in the beginning, and then gradually decrease the width.

— Start with simple exercises, and only later create challenges.

— Before starting calmness training, build trust and gain confidence with leading exercises.

— Start every training session with leading exercises.

— Always walk between frightening obstacles and the horse.

— Keep an eye on other horses in the area.

— Start the exercises at the halt.

— The horse is allowed to explore any object first; then the handler should lead him past it at a walk.

GROUNDWORK IN ACTION

Sample Exercises for Training—and Fun

GROUNDWORK IS FUN!

The goal of groundwork is to achieve nuanced, harmonious interaction with the horse, where the horse solves all challenges with an attentive, willing, and trusting attitude, and he is centered around his own inner balance and content with his tasks. This learned behavior of the horse is also referred to as "good manners."

FAIRNESS FIRST

It is not just the horse who has to learn to "behave." The handler must also continue to work on herself and further her own education in order to know exactly how to act appropriately, fairly and correctly towards the horse in all kinds of situations.

THE GROUNDWORK AREA

Groundwork should be conducted in a fenced-in area or riding arena. Only when the horse is consistently confident is it possible to include training sessions out on the trail. Especially with younger horses, working in a small group provides a sense of safety. However, the size of the group must match the size of the activity area to ensure that a safe distance between horses (about 13 feet / 4 meters) can be always maintained. Ill-mannered, hot horses should be handled alone by experienced handlers to avoid endangering other humans or equines.

A quiet environment makes it easier for the horse to focus on his handler.

EQUIPMENT FOR THE HORSE

The equipment must be appropriate, consist of the right materials, and be suitably fitted to the horse. You must be able to apply the aids in an appropriately goal-oriented way.

Well suited for groundwork: sturdy, level sand footing, with a border.

DIFFERENT TYPES OF GROUNDWORK

Options

Groundwork includes different areas of application with specific focus.

— Daily handling of the horse in all areas
— Groundwork with a lead rope
— Work at a distance
— Groundwork without a lead rope
— Liberty work in the round pen
— Longeing
— Long-reining, which also serves as preparation for driving
— In-hand work (collected lessons)
— Agility training

People learn to ...

— Communicate clearly and safely with the horse
— Act consistently in their daily interactions with the horse
— Optimize the application of their aids
— Interpret the individual behavior of horses more accurately
— React in problematic situations more appropriately and with better success

Groundwork helps to ...

— Support the rider from the ground up (beginning riders/young horses)
— Teach new exercises like a turn-on-the-forehand, leg yield, or rein-back
— Prepare for longeing, loading or driving

Groundwork serves as ...

— A diversion
— An alternative to riding
— A warm-up before riding for rider and horse

Too much can be just as bad as too little, which can also cause strong defensive behavior. Groundwork is usually done with a rope halter or with a well-fitted leather or nylon halter without fleece padding.

For some exercises, however, a bridle is also an option. Here, the whip can be used as a supportive driving aid. It's a good idea to use boots to protect horses' legs, especially when working over poles.

Never tie a horse in a rope halter. Even though the material of the halter might look light and thin, it's tear-resistant—so much so that if the horse tries to pull free, it can cause serious injuries.

HALTER

The halter should fit well, and preferably be adjustable at poll and chin to allow for the best possible fit for the horse. The noseband should sit two or three finger-widths below the horse's cheekbone, like an English noseband. If the halter sits too low and the horse pulls against it, or the handler uses too much force on the lead rope, the halter can cause pain and injury to the horse in the area where the nasal bone turns into sensitive cartilage. The noseband must leave enough room for the horse to move his jaw in a chewing motion without obstruction.

Slide the crownpiece from above through the loop, and then bring it under the loop towards the front of the horse's face ...

... before bringing the tip of the rope back toward the horse's tail ...

... and tying it off into a knot. Repeat one more time above the first knot.

Bring the tail of the rope below and toward the front of the horse, and pull it through above the first knot.

ROPE HALTER

A rope halter, when used and adjusted correctly, allows for a very precise but subtle application of aids to the horse, which is why it is often used.

These halters are created out of a thin rope, shaped into a halter with a series of knots. The knots are positioned along the flat parts of the horse's face, so they don't create any specific pressure points—as long as the rope you are using doesn't have a diameter of more than about a quarter of an inch.

Fitting a rope halter: The noseband should sit around two or three finger-widths below the cheekbone, and must be loose enough to allow the horse to chew and yawn unobstructed. There cannot be any knots pressing against the nasal bone. The cheekpieces need to be long enough that you can close the halter along the line of the throat and ensure it can't slide down. This part serves as the throatlatch. The poll piece is always tied with a double knot that sits snugly but can easily be undone by the handler.

The left hand is holding the rest of the coiled-up lead rope.

A leather halter that fits well, used with a lead rope and halter clip.

Quick-release snap and halter clip.

LEAD ROPE (6½-12 FEET)

Any rope that is a minimum of 6½ feet (2 meters) long and fitted on one end with a halter snap or similar snap is potentially suitable as a lead rope. A quick-release snap on the end of a lead rope can open too easily when used incorrectly, which makes it inappropriate. The material the lead rope is made of should be somewhat thick, with a substantial feel in the hand. It shouldn't be stretchy. The right length will vary depending on your goals, but it should be somewhere between 8–12 feet (2.5–3.5 meters). The rope should be long enough to provide some leeway for the horse to move, especially a big horse. The tail end of the lead rope can have a leather popper attached.

LEAD ROPE (10-15 FEET)

You should also have a longer lead rope (½ inch in diameter) that is made of a solid core with a braided polyester exterior. This gives the rope a comfortable weight and allows for greater precision. Pure cotton is very soft and stretches easily, and its low weight makes it less accurate in giving aids. The length you should use depends on the horse; 10 feet (3.5 meters) is recommended for ordinary horses, with up to 15 feet (4.8 meters) for bigger horses. When handling young, hot-blooded horses, make sure you have a lead rope or lunge line that's at least 22 feet (7 meters) long so you can keep the horse at a safe distance. It's also worth getting a lead rope with a leather popper at the tail end that can be used as a forward driving aid. The leather popper creates a buzzing sound, and it feels softer when it touches the horse's body than the loose end of an ordinary rope. For a horse, the tail end of a lead rope is also easier to see than the thin leather or nylon string of a lunge whip.

WHIPS

When working the horse in a bridle, a whip about 3–4 feet (1 to 1.3 meters) long, a short lunge whip with a leather or rope lash, or a driving whip can be used.

The whip is used as an aid for tactile cues, not as a punishment.

EQUIPMENT FOR THE HUMAN

When you are caring for a horse, small changes in the feel of his skin, like bruises and scrapes or inflammation in the limbs, are more easily detected without gloves. Often, the earliest stages of an injury can be detected that way, and quick action can be taken accordingly. When leading, lungeing, and working at a distance, however, gloves need to be worn to avoid injuries to your hands if the horse suddenly bolts.

Sturdy, ankle-high boots or riding boots protect the feet. Sneakers and sandals are inappropriate footwear for working around horses. It should go without saying that a riding helmet should be worn by everyone,

especially children and teenagers, and those handlers who are working with spirited horses or stallions.

TASKS ON THE GROUND

Anything that involves one of the many different interactions with the horse from the ground is groundwork, meaning everything that is part of the daily handling of the horse out of the saddle:

— Greeting and approaching the horse
— Haltering and grooming
— Bridling and tacking
— Leading
— Work from a distance
— Long-lining
— Preparation for driving
— Longeing
— Working over poles
— Agility work
— Bombproofing
— Groundwork without lines
— Liberty work

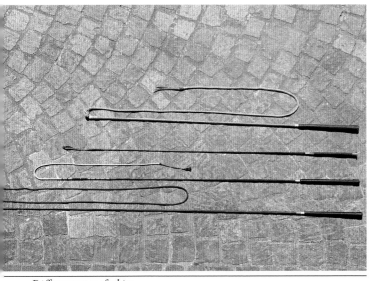

Different types of whips.

Lead rope with halter clip and leather popper.

19

The horse is trustingly turning towards the handler in his stall, which is a good start for the session.

When putting on the halter, the ears are gently pushed underneath the crownpiece one at a time, and then the throatlatch is snapped shut.

GREETING AND APPROACHING

When I get a horse from the stall, paddock, or field, I must approach him at an angle from the front, on his left side. At the same time, I greet him softly and kindly, yet clearly, and I pay attention to his facial expressions and the movement of his ears. If the horse is busy eating or distracted by his pasture mates, I make sure he is aware of my presence and looks at me before I touch him on the neck. I don't want to startle him. I don't approach the horse from behind, in case he turns around in his stall; instead, I pause in the doorway and address him from there. Only when he looks at me with a friendly expression do I approach further.

Leading the horse out of his stall to the right, with a fully open stall door.

The narrow barn aisle requires focus to keep the horse from bumping into anything.

Horses should turn toward the person with a friendly demeanor when they enter the stall. This is a sign of a trusting relationship and indicates that the horse enjoys being with and working with humans. Horses that are going through an adjustment period in a new environment and still have their guard up might benefit from a greeting ritual with a small treat (a piece of carrot or apple).

HALTERING

To halter the horse, position yourself next to the horse's neck, facing his head. When using a halter without a poll closure, open the throatlatch and reach with your right hand from below, around the horse's head. Pull the noseband carefully over the horse's nose and the crownpiece over the horse's ears, and then buckle the halter. If the horse raises his head while you're haltering him, block the bridge of the nose from moving upward with your hand. It's easier if the horse has learned to lower his head and practically slips into the halter on his own.

The halter should offer enough room around the poll to allow the crownpiece to be pulled up easily over the horse's ears with both hands. If the horse is very sensitive around the ears, use a halter that can be unbuckled at the crownpiece. Slip the noseband over his nose as described above, and then take the crownpiece and place it with your right hand across the horse's poll, staying clear of the horse's ears. Then close the buckle on the left side of the horse's head.

The noseband of the halter should sit about two to three finger-widths below the cheekbones. If it sits too low and rests on the part of the horse's nose that is made of cartilage, it can cause injuries and pain; if it sits too high, it causes discomfort around the cheekbones.

BARN AND GROOMING AREA

It's a good idea to always lead the horse with a rope, whether you're going from his stall or paddock to the grooming area, or taking him from the field back to the barn. Leading by the halter, without a rope, leaves you without real control in the event the horse spooks or just raises his head too high for you to reach. Getting your arm jerked up or your fingers or hand pinched between the halter and the horse's head can cause significant injuries.

The lead rope should be clipped to the halter on the lower middle ring with a halter snap. Take the rope with your whole hand anywhere from 8 to 20 inches below the buckle, in a relaxed grip. The thumb of your lead hand should be pointing toward the horse's head. Inside the barn, it's okay to lead the horse on a tie rope with a panic snap. However, in any outdoor areas, leading should always be done with a longer lead rope and a halter snap, which won't easily open by accident.

When leading through stall doors or tight barn doors, always go in front of the horse so you won't get caught between the door frame and the horse. Make sure the horse stays diagonally behind you.

In the barn aisle, the handler typically walks on the left side of the horse, slightly behind the horse's head. When leading the horse into his stall, you should always turn him around to face the stall door. Only then should you take off the halter. This way, you avoid getting stuck in a corner of the stall behind the horse.

Encourage the horse to lower his head by massaging the poll area with your fingertips.

As soon as the horse starts to lower his head, the tactile cue goes away.

TYING UP

In the grooming area, the horse should be tied up to one ring or crosstied with two ropes, one on either side. Both options must first be practiced with the horse. The tie ring should be firmly anchored and attached at least at shoulder height, and the rope should be 2–3 feet long so the horse isn't limited in his ability to raise his neck and head freely, especially when he's frightened. Too short a rope can cause a frightened horse to try and break away, which will endanger both horse and human and can lead to injuries.

When using crossties, the ropes should be attached at shoulder height or higher. The length of both ropes should allow the horse to move his head and neck freely. At the same time, the ropes must not be so long that the horse can step into them or get his head caught under them. Tying is always done with a safety knot, and the rope needs to have a panic snap to allow for a quick release in an emergency.

Never tie a horse to moving structures like doors, gates, or railings. A horse can only be tied inside his stall if he is friendly with his neighbors. Otherwise, horse quarrels can create dangerous situations for the person inside the stall.

Only use a leather halter to tie the horse, and *never* the bridle, rope halter, or cavesson.

BRIDLING

It's a good idea to practice leading the horse with a bridle. Bridling is similar to putting on the halter (see page 21). Stand on the left side of the horse, next to his head, and release the tie rope first. Then place the reins over the upper part of the horse's neck to prevent him from getting away once the halter has been taken off. The halter should be hung up or safely set aside to prevent anybody from stepping into it. Then, reach with your right arm from below around the horse's head, and put your right hand on the bridge of his nose to keep his head in position. The bridle should be gathered in your right hand around the cheek pieces. The bit sits in your left hand, and is held to the horse's front teeth, without touching them. If the horse doesn't open his mouth on his own, the thumb of the left hand puts pressure on the bar or corner of the horse's mouth.

Slide the bit into the horse's mouth with your left hand, while your right hand lifts the crownpiece up to prevent the bit from being spit back out. Once your left hand is free, use it to grasp the bridle by the crownpiece and lift it over the horse's right ear, by folding the ear to the front with your right hand. Use your left hand to lift the crownpiece over the left ear, too, which should also be guided forward to pass under the crownpiece by your right hand. This way, you avoid getting the horse's ears stuck underneath the crownpiece. Make sure you also smooth the mane and forelock out from under the crownpiece. This step is especially important for sensitive horses. Then buckle the throatlatch, allowing space for one fist to fit between the leather and the horse's throat. The intent of the throatlatch is to prevent the bridle from accidentally slipping off. After that, buckle the noseband and, if applicable, the flash of the bridle. When taking off the bridle, reverse the order in which you unbuckle the straps.

If the horse raises his head when you're trying to put on his bridle, you should first work on teaching him to lower it. Put your right hand on his poll, behind his ears, and apply gentle pressure to ask him to lower his head.

Checklist
FOR LEAD TRAINING IN INDOOR AND OUTDOOR ARENAS

....

❏ The space is fenced in.

❏ No riders are present in the arena.

❏ Distracting factors are eliminated as much as possible.

❏ You are training with small group of 2 to 4 horses, depending on the training level of the horses and the size of the arena, for a total of 6 horses at the most.

❏ You are maintaining safe distance between the horses: 2 horse lengths (13–20 feet / 4–6 meters).

❏ The horses' need for movement has been satisfied in advance—through turnout in a field or paddock, or moderate riding or longeing that did not demand too much (conserving the horses' ability to concentrate).

❏ You have not wrapped the lead line, longe line, or reins around your hands. You have gathered any excess into loops of at least 16 inches in diameter.

❏ You have opened the horses' reins up at the buckle to avoid any risk of either human or horse stepping into them.

❏ You are going to start with simple exercises.

❏ You have ensured that horses and handlers suit each other's level of training: Inexperienced handlers require safe, reliable horses to build trust and confidence; inexperienced horses require experienced handlers for guidance.

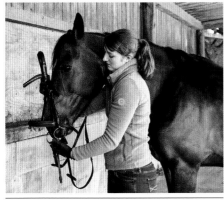

The right hand keeps the horse's head in a vertical position.

Valencia is waiting in a relaxed posture until everything is buckled up correctly.

While you're leading with the horse in a bridle ...

Wearing appropriate show clothes is part of any riding te

... the reins should be held coiled up.

LEADING WITH A BRIDLE

While leading, the reins should be held with your right hand, anywhere from 10–20 inches below the bit rings, separated by one or two fingers. The left rein should be held between your thumb and index finger, and the right rein between your middle and ring finger. The reins should then be folded over once or twice in the right hand. The buckle at the end of the reins should be open. Children can also carry the ends of the reins in their left hands, to keep them from dragging on the ground.

When leading with a bridle, cues to the horse from your voice and body language are particularly important. Carrying a whip to help with forward driving aids is an option. However, your use of the whip should be purposeful and limited to avoid conditioning the horse to orient himself primarily by cues from the whip. The whip is used as a driving aid with a touch right behind the horse's shoulder. As soon as the horse gives the correct response, the whip should be lowered and carried passively at the handler's side.

As a restraining aid, the whip can be used with a touch to the front of the shoulder—never with a touch to either the neck or head of the horse. The meaning of this cue is first established at the halt. Here, when cued with the whip, the horse should shift his center of gravity backward and eventually take half a step back. Using restraining aids on a forward-thinking horse for the first time doesn't usually yield success right away, as the horse hasn't understood the aid yet. Slowing the pace is a skill that needs to be taught in peace and with patience.

Additional restraining aids include a combination of body language, voice input, and cues from the reins to the bit to the whip—only as a last resort, and only if necessary.

PASSING OTHER HORSES

When leading horses past each other in a barn aisle, there are rules that need to be followed to avoid injuries to both humans and horses. There are definitely horses who don't like each other or who show distinct gender behaviors and follow patterns in their interactions with each other. They may try to bite or kick. No matter the situation, it's important to pass other horses swiftly, interpret their body language accurately, and act accordingly. Ears pinned back and a tight mouth are obvious signs of "moodiness." Horses should not be allowed to sniff each other, and a safe distance needs to be maintained.

Make sure to take notice of any lifting of or threatening movements with the hind legs. This can easily lead to an attack on a passing horse. Clear, confident management of this behavior by the handler will usually diffuse the situation. Otherwise, adding a second set of helping hands might be a good idea.

Firmly and swiftly leading horses past each other on a straight line, with sufficient space between them.

The black mare is watching curiously to see who's coming toward her from behind. Nevertheless, she's supposed to remain at a halt.

Leading in the correct position, slightly behind the horse's head.

Leading at the girth, showing how you would secure a hypothetical rider.

POSITIONS TO LEAD FROM NEXT TO THE HORSE

— Behind the horse's head, right by his poll. Keeping the lead rope short allows for precise guidance (for example, through tight turns, as for a maze exercise) and it helps you regulate the pace with excited horses.

— In the middle of the horse's neck, right in front of the shoulders, with a longer lead rope. This is a good position from which to direct driving aids towards the horse's girth. It's also an appropriate position for horses who already respond well to body language.

— Next to the girth. This is a good position when you are leading insecure riders or small children; it provides added safety and gives you the chance to intervene quickly.

— Next to the hindquarters. This position is only recommended for very experienced handlers and well-trained horses who are working on lateral movements. (In this position, boisterous horses or horses who are still inconsistent in their behavior can cause injuries when kicking or bolting.)

LEADING WITH PRECISION

When leading a horse, you should not just pull him along behind you. As a preliminary step before any other activities with the horse (riding, driving, and so on), you should walk next to the horse in a position that lets you apply both restraining and forward driving aids. This way, you can influence the tempo, eagerness, and direction of the horse. In the most basic position, the handler walks half an arm's length away, positioned next to the horse's neck and right behind his head. Leading from here, done well, looks easy and natural.

The horse should be led on a slightly slack lead rope, with his pace and the direction of his movement guided by the handler, who should walk confidently and with clear body language on the intended line. The handler must adjust the rhythm of her own motion to that of the horse, which results in unity of movement. Matching the horse's rhythm this way allows the handler to apply the aids easily, and to begin with the lightest possible pressure. Both driving and restraining aids must always coordinate with the movement pattern of the horse's legs if you want him to respond smoothly. During the push-off phase of his stride, a driving or restraining cue should be communicated to the corresponding leg to allow him to move in good balance. A slight bend forward in the handler's body and shifting of the handler's weight onto the leg with which she's stepping forward signals to the horse that he must walk on. The handler moving into an energetic walk causes the horse to walk along eagerly. Likewise, stepping into a trot should encourage the horse to start trotting as well, and a switch to the rhythm of the canter serves as a canter aid for experienced horses. Even at beginner levels, this can be a valuable tool for teaching the horse to canter.

HALTING AND STANDING

Naturally, part of leading is practicing how to halt. First, the halt must be initiated from the walk with restraining aids. When you are cueing with the lead rope or the reins, it's important to focus on keeping the horse straight; otherwise, he will tend to swerve to the outside with his hindquarters. The application of aids through the lead rope or reins should noticeably decrease as you and your horse become more proficient with leading techniques. With some practice, even halting from a trot will be a success.

Use voice cues ("whoa" or "brrrr") to prepare the horse to halt. You should always use the same cue. Then delay the rhythm of your movement, staying slightly behind with your upper body; shift your weight to your standing leg; and allow your other leg to join it to arrive in a square halt. The horse is supposed to execute this halt in the same way. To get a square halt from the horse, you have to pay attention to the horse's balance. Too much pressure on the halter or the horse's head usually results in the horse hanging on your hand—and a crooked halt. If the horse doesn't respond to your body language and the subtle cues from the halter, a touch with the rope to the horse's shoulder area can serve as a more direct cue to halt or slow down. Again, the intensity of the cue should increase until the horse gives a good response. Do not surprise the horse with your cues! When leading with a bridle and using a whip as a supporting tool, you must first teach the horse the meaning of the cue, or the meaning of the whip's end cap against his shoulder, in small stages.

STANDING OBEDIENTLY

Quiet and obedient standing (for several minutes) should be possible for every horse. It must be part of any groundwork training program. Initially, it should be used to provide a moment of relaxation after a movement exercise, always in the same spot and next to a quiet neighbor. The horse will feel secure with a friend or a group standing nearby, and will think of the halt as a reward. A voice cue can support this request—for example, "Hoooo," or, "Haaaalt." It must always be the same cue. Should the horse step sideways in the halt, he should be quickly redirected to his original spot, followed once more by the voice cue and praise for him during the halt.

If the horse does not yet respond reliably to the handler's body language, the end of the lead rope or a whip can be used in addition to the handler's voice.

In the halt, this horse is standing straight.

Backing up with a cue from the whip at the point of the shoulder.

A well-coordinated play of rein aids, whip cue, and body language results in a nice diagonal rein-back.

REIN-BACK

Backing up a horse is needed in various everyday situations, and should therefore be a well-practiced maneuver. It also serves as a valuable exercise for the horse's suppleness and throughness in the implementation of the aids. At first, it will take the horse some willpower to overcome his hesitation about stepping precisely into that area behind his body where he cannot see. For this reason, horses need to learn that they can trust their handler to back them up safely, in small stages. This exercise should never be misused as punishment. Praising the horse for each backward step improves his suppleness and responsiveness to the aids.

First, the horse should halt quietly and calmly, and stand square with a slightly lowered, relaxed neck. Then the handler should turn around to face the horse and stand next to the horse's head. The handler stands upright and moves as if to take a step toward the horse's shoulder. At the same time, a voice cue—for example, "Baaack"—is given. This exercise should always have the same cue. Practicing this movement teaches the horse to better balance his own body. The input of the handler plays a big role. She must not push forcefully or use her own body to try to move the horse, but rather must achieve the goal of the exercise with a precise application of the aids. The cue to back is always directed towards the leg that is pushing off, not the standing leg.

As the training of the horse continues, the handler remains standing parallel to the horse. On straight lines, the handler walks backward with the horse, facing the same direction as the horse. Shift your center of gravity backwards, give a voice cue, and and signal at the halter or at the point of the horse's shoulder and then step backward at the same time as the horse.

MOVING OFF IN THE WALK

To start leading, the handler should take the lead rope with the right hand anywhere from 8–16 inches below the snap and then ask the horse with a voice cue (clucking), in combination with body language, to move forward. Body language is supposed to encourage the horse to move forward in step with the handler. The voice cue prepares the horse and prompts him to walk on. During the voice cue, the handler shifts her weight and walks forward at the same time as the horse. If at first the horse does not react in a timely manner, you can shorten the lead rope temporarily to a hold right underneath the snap and guide the horse's head slightly forward.

Then, repeat the voice cues for the walk-on command. The next increase in the application of the aids will be a tactile cue through touch. Forward driving aids are applied with the end of the lead rope or with the whip by gently touching the horse directly behind his shoulder until he walks forward. At that moment, the forward aid is reduced and then reapplied as needed until the horse gives the appropriate response. Releasing the tactile cues in combination with vocal praise signals to the horse that he is doing the right thing.

When leading on the right side of the horse, the end of the lead rope is carried in the right hand and the relevant cues are given with the left hand.

Trying to lead the horse by simply pulling on the rope can cause strong negative reactions in him. The horse is always stronger than you. Horses that are still nervous or do not listen to you consistently should never be led on a short lead rope, as it is very easy for them to rip the rope right out of your hand when they jump away. This can lead to injuries to your hand, arm, and shoulder.

Work with a shorter lead rope to make it easier for you to give well-timed cues. The end of the lead rope can swing softly forward or touch the point of shoulder, as added cues. These supporting aids should decrease to the point where a practiced horse-handler team can do the exercise with only body language as the cue.

Once the horse shifts his balance to his hindquarters, a touch to the point of the shoulder with your hand, the lead rope, or the knob of the whip can initiate the step backward. Initially, the horse should immediately receive praise once the first backing step is taken. Then, bit by bit, you will ask for more backward steps. The horse should step back diagonally and remain supple in his topline throughout the exercise. He should not push back with stiff legs. If he does that, this exercise is no longer helping you build his trust.

If the horse moves his haunches sideways, there are several options for correction:

— Straighten the horse's head or direct him to the side to which he is moving his haunches.

— Create a visual border with your hand, the lead rope, or the whip on the side that is stepping out.

— Halt the horse on the track and let him back up along the rail.

For insecure horses, it's easier to start working on backing up in an open area rather than a confined space. Initially, it's all about giving confident, solid aids during your rein-back practice. Only when more trust has been established are horses willing to back up between objects.

As guidance for more inexperienced handlers, the following exercises can be helpful:

— Backing up through a chute of cones.

— Backing up in between two ground poles.

Praising the horse for standing quietly.

To switch sides, take one step forward ...

... then turn around in front of the horse, and ...

... gather the reins in the other hand.

LEADING AT THE WALK

At first, the handler leads her horse along the track while walking on the inside, to be able to lead on a straight line. However, if there are distractions positioned to the outside, like a grandstand, people, or noises, the handler should walk between these disturbances and the horse but maintain enough distance from the rail or fence to avoid getting pinned against it. I recommend keeping a six- to ten-foot distance from the track.

When leading, the personal space of both handler and horse must be respected and observed, which means keeping a consistent distance of about 20 inches between the two of you. With an unruly horse, an inexperienced handler will reflexively tend to try to manage the horse's speed by pushing her own body into the horse's shoulder.

That's not a solution, and usually does not result in the desired outcome. The goal of groundwork is to shape the communication

Intentionally initiating the walk with the mare Balluca: Walking on in step with each other, with a voice cue and body language.

between handler and horse in a way that allows the horse to react calmly, obediently, and with trust to the subtle cues of the handler. These cues are: body language, voice, and the tactile aids with halter, bridle, lead rope, or whip.

SWITCHING SIDES AND LEADING FROM EITHER SIDE

Along with the traditional position where you are leading with the right hand, switching and leading from the other side is part of this training as well. Horses should be

exercised on both sides equally, and no one side should be overtaxed by exercising it too long. Switching sides becomes necessary when there is a chance of the horse spooking and jeopardizing the handler's safety. Outside factors could cause the handler to be run over by a spooking horse (for example, fear of waving tarps, spectators, or noise from a grandstand).

If she can switch sides at any time, the handler is able to take herself out of a danger zone, and her confidence in the maneuver, if it is well-practiced, will give the horse assurance and courage in the face of whatever sources of stress are upsetting him.

Start by practicing a switch to the other side at the halt. The handler should stand on the left side of the horse and face in the same direction as the horse. She should then cue the horse to halt and stand, and take a big step forward and sideways with her right leg in front of the horse, turning on that same leg halfway so she is now facing the horse. The left leg is then brought over to the new side of the horse, arriving once again in a forward-facing position, now standing on the right side of the horse.

The switch from the right side to the left side of the horse is initiated and carried out with the left leg forward. With some practice, changing sides like this can be done during forward movement. However, your cues to the horse before and after the switch are important. Shorten your pace and the length of your steps to ensure that a well-trained and attentive horse doesn't misinterpret your swift forward steps as an instruction to speed up.

From a right bend, straightening, and then switching to a left bend.

CHANGE OF BEND IN THE WALK

Horses must adjust their pace to match their handlers. This skill is first acquired at the walk. To start with, the handler should learn to change the horse's pace with her input. Forward aids are communicated through heightened body tension, meaning a straightening of the upper body and an energetic, engaged walk. If the horse doesn't respond, reinforcing cues like a touch with the end of the lead rope or the whip are added until the desired pace is reached. These cues are not the same, nor continuous, but rather are applied with different intensity, either to increase or to pause. To reduce the pace of the walk, the handler reduces her own speed, her upper body falls slightly behind, and she gives a halting voice cue like, "Hoooah," as well as a restraining signal with the lead rope.

WEAVING

Weaving means leading the horse in shallow bending lines around a set number of poles or cones. Horse and handler should become one unit and walk with even speed and direction.

In a turn to the right, the handler walks a little further up, close to the horse's head. The horse is supposed to move to the right and adjust the flexion of his poll and neck, and

Evenly bent to the left, using body language to prepare the horse for the bend to the right.

ideally the bend through his barrel as well, to match the bending lines of the weaving pattern.

The handler also rotates slightly through her entire body, to the right. She should walk upright along the intended line, with confidence and purpose, and restrict the path of the horse with her own posture. If necessary, her left hand or arm can help define the track more clearly with a tap of the lead rope or whip against the horse's left shoulder. Swing the lead rope with your left hand behind your back in the direction of or against the horse's shoulder. With a little practice, the simple movement of your arm backward will be enough, and the horse will respond to this cue as readily as if you had touched him.

In the left turn, the handler turns slightly to the left and stays a little farther back, right in front of the horse's shoulder. The horse is supposed to bend to the left in the left turn and adjust his barrel to the bending line of the weaving pattern. The handler should encourage the horse forward, as he has a little bit more ground to cover.

She must also pay attention and not allow the horse to start trailing behind her, as that poses the risk of the horse stepping up too close to her feet and causing injuries. Especially in the left-hand turn, it's important to consistently maintain a safe distance between handler and horse.

The horse is trotting willingly in-hand. Caroline and Candira are facing straight ahead, Caroline leading with her right hand. The distance maintained between them is big enough for them to avoid bumping into each other.

Candira is responding attentively to Caroline's preparations for the halt. Caroline has the correct timing; her body language and voice are signaling to Candira in unison.

TROTTING IN A STRAIGHT LINE

From time to time, there are situations where the horse needs to be trotted in-hand—for example, for a health check, for the evaluation before a sale, for a presentation, and so on. Therefore, this movement should be practiced with your horse. First, however, you should be able to reliably perform changes of bend at the walk (page 32). To transition into the trot, the driving cues of voice, body language, and possibly touch with lead rope or whip are increased. The handler takes faster, shorter steps, and eventually starts to trot herself to arrive at the same rhythm as the horse.

It is important for the transition to the trot to happen calmly. As soon as there is too much pressure on the horse, he might start to run forward to escape the control of the handler, especially if she is inexperienced.

You should choose the speed of the trot so it is easy for you to keep up with the horse. In the beginning, extension in the trot is not needed. What is important is demonstrating a rhythmic, smooth, supple trot from which a transition to the walk or halt is possible at any time. The horse must always remain straight.

CHANGING SPEED

Changing speed within a gait on the ground should be smooth and supple, just as it would be if you were riding or driving. The handler must walk with good posture, and the rhythm of her movement should match the horse's. She must prepare for the change in advance and keep the horse's attention with voice cues and body language in a way that looks as if hardly any cues are being given. However, changes in speed will only be successful if the handler takes her cues from the movement of the horse. The forward driving aids are given in the same way as when you ask the horse to walk on, but are adjusted to prompt a change in speed.

— Use your voice and body language: keep center of gravity forward, and walk more energetically.

— Apply forward driving aids by swinging the lead rope or touching the girth area with it, or by using the whip to touch the area around the horse's girth.

— Remember that restraining aids will only appear skillful and invisible if they are in sync with the movement of the horse.

— Always cue the swinging leg. Shift your own center of gravity slightly backwards, put more weight onto the heel of your foot, and reduce your speed. This aid can be supported with voice cues.

It is important for the horse to remain straight forward or straight on the intended line of travel. Otherwise, the horse walks crooked, and, as in riding and driving, that will result in tension in the horse's body.

CHANGING GAIT

To change from one gait to another, the leader must indicate the rhythm of the intended gait. To transition from walk to trot you apply driving aids with your voice and the rope or whip to the horse's barrel until both of you are in the trot. The horse must trust you and must have learned to respond to the driving aids. With a pony or a very slow trotting horse the leader can remain walking but does indicate the new rhythm through their aids. That also applies to canter. Here the horse must be further along in its training and must be able to canter quite slowly. During the trainings phase the horse will progress faster if the leader's movement mirrors the beat of the desired gait.

YIELDING THE FOREHAND

When the horse is yielding his forehand, the forehand moves sideways, and the haunches keep moving in place. This exercise is needed in everyday handling as well—for example, when maneuvering into a grooming area.

The handler should stand directly in front of the horse's shoulder, facing the croup when handling inexperienced horses and facing the head when handling more seasoned horses.

With a shortened lead rope, the handler gives a slight press in the intended direction of the sideways movement while also paying attention to the shift of the horse's weight, as that will make it easier to give cues at the right moments. Then the handler allows the horse to take several steps to the side.

Executed correctly, this turn may be a quarter turn (90°), a half turn (180°), a three-quarter turn (270°), or a full turn (360°). While the forehand is stepping sideways, the poll is flexed slightly opposite the direction of movement. The front legs are crossing in front of each other. The hind legs are stepping in a small circle or in place. With some practice, the handler should be able to match the sequence of the horse's steps, and be able to suspend his sideways movement at any time.

YIELDING THE HAUNCHES

Yielding the haunches is needed in everyday handling of the horse and makes it easier to learn the turn-on-the-forehand in the future. The handler positions herself by the girth area next to the horse, looking toward the hindquarters. A cue toward the barrel invites the horse to step sideways with his hindquarters. This cue can be a tap with the finger, a swing of the lead rope, or a touch with the whip. As soon as the horse reacts, the cue stops, and is only repeated for the next request. The hind legs are supposed to cross each other; the forehand remains, stepping in place. You should be able to pause this movement after each step. The horse must respond promptly to your forward and halting cues and not take over the movement and make it his own.

If the horse acts before you apply a cue, he appears motivated and willing to learn. But down the road, this can result in unwanted shifting of the haunches every time you look at or walk towards the hindquarters of the horse, which could cause problems during grooming or tacking. So if this happens, you must correct the horse's overzealous motivation. It's easiest to avoid having to worry about it by teaching movement and halt equally, and in small stages.

YIELDING LATERALLY

Yielding laterally can prepare the horse for leg yields, as well as for aligning the horse under saddle. It should follow the previous exercises.

This exercise is done on both sides. First, the handler stands next to the horse by his shoulder, facing the haunches. She holds the horse on a relatively short lead rope or rein to be able to lead and flex the horse with clear, precise cues. As during riding, the horse is counter-flexed through the poll, followed by the application of a lateral aid in the direction of movement.

Forward movement is initiated with a clucking voice signal, and is supported by a forward driving cue with the right arm, which can include a touch with the lead rope or the whip to the horse's barrel or haunches.

The prompt should not be directed toward the flank, as that can cause some horses to react sensitively or defensively.

At first, start with short sequences of lateral steps, until the horse and handler are sufficiently secure in this part of the exercise. The horse is to go forward and sideways with regular crossing of both front and hind legs. As during the previous exercise, you must be able to pause the movement of the horse at any moment. The horse must not anticipate the aids, learn to evade the handler, or fall out over the outside shoulder. In addition, the horse must learn to stop when a cue with the lead rope or whip is applied from the left to the outside shoulder or over the back to the point of the hip. Only then does this exercise have true value. Should the handler have gained enough experience to face and walk forward with the horse in the direction of travel, she once again must make sure the horse doesn't fall out over the shoulder. For that reason, this exercise should be supplemented with stretches of simple straight walks.

The handler should imagine an exact line (straight or diagonal) along which she wants to ask the horse for the lateral steps. This allows the handler to more reliably determine how far the horse needs to step over. In the beginning, this will be fewer steps than after several training sessions. Horses become more secure in their balance during lateral movement as their suppleness increases. From here, you can continue developing this exercise into lateral steps over a ground pole, and then into the half-pass. In the half-pass, the horse is flexed and bent in the direction of travel and noticeably carries more weight with the hind leg.

The initial cues for yielding of the haunches, carried out with lead rope and whip.

The hind legs cross; the front legs move in place.

A good finish: the horse is standing straight and almost square on all four legs.

LEADING THE HORSE THROUGH SCHOOL FIGURES

The warm-up phase before riding offers a great opportunity for learning by leading from the ground. In this scenario, the horse is bridled, and you are leading him through the different school figures. It's helpful to use cones as visual markers for handler and horse when working on serpentines, circles, volte, teardrop turns, back to the track, and many others. School figures are ideal as individual exercises or during a lesson as group drills, but in this setting will require being led with big safe distances between teams. School figures are also some of the skills required for the horse management section of the Pony Club Standards of Proficiency (SOPs).

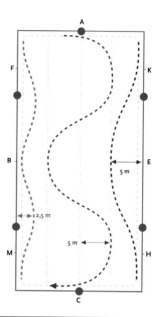

Green: two-loop serpentine, distance to first track 8 feet (2.5 meters).
Red: serpentine, 3 loops, distance to centerline 16 feet (5 meters).
Blue: one-loop serpentine, distance to first track 16 feet (5 meters).

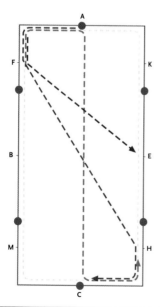

School figures with change of rein.
Green: change of rein down centerline.
Red: change of rein on the long diagonal.
Blue: change of rein on the short diagonal.

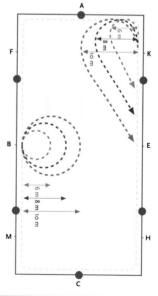

Volte and half circle back to the track.
Green: 10 meters (33 feet) in diameter.
Red: 8 meters (26 feet) in diameter.
Orange: 6 meters (20 feet) in diameter.

☞ EXERCISE 1: WALK VARIATIONS

This is an example of school figures with walk variations.

1. Enter at a walk, leading with the right hand on the left side of the horse, and proceed at the walk.

2. Change of rein on the short diagonal; working walk.

3. Slow walk.

4. Medium walk.

5. Volte, 10 meters in diameter.

6. Halt and switch the side you're leading from.

7. Change of rein on long diagonal; working walk.

8. Halt, rein back 5 steps; proceed in medium walk.

9. Switch the side you're leading from during the movement.

10. Down centerline; slow walk.

11. Working walk.

12. Halt, and end the exercise.

FIGURES AND DIMENSIONS
— Volte: 10 meters (33 feet) in diameter

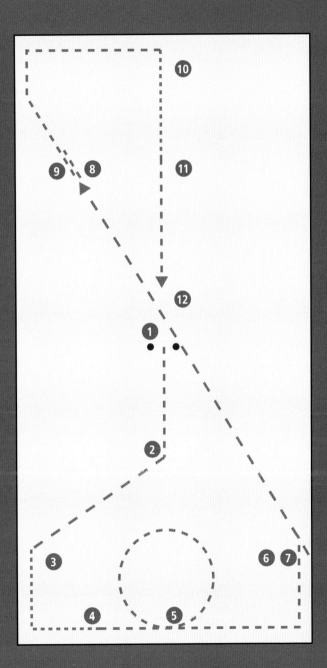

☞ EXERCISE 2: SCHOOL FIGURES

This is a sample exercise for school figures in the working walk.

1. Enter at a walk, leading with the right hand on the left side of the horse, and proceed at the walk.

2. Go down the centerline at a working walk.

3. Track left.

4. One-loop serpentine.

5. Volte, 10 meters in diameter.

6. Circle, one and a half laps.

7. Change of rein from circle to circle.

8. Circle, one lap.

9. Four-loop serpentine.

10. Change of rein on the short diagonal.

11. Turn right.

12. Halt, and end the exercise.

FIGURES AND DIMENSIONS
— Volte: 10 meters (33 feet) in diameter

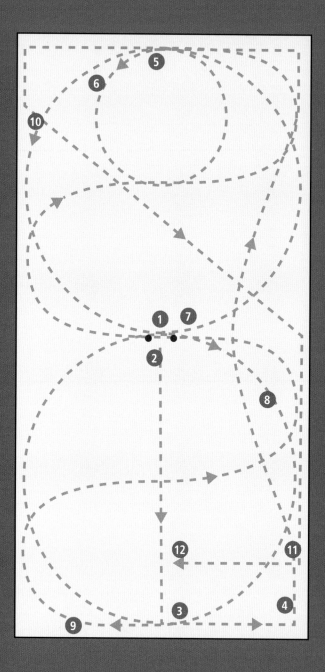

☞ EXERCISE 3: LATERAL MOVEMENTS

This is a sample exercise for lateral movements in the walk and trot.

1. Enter at a walk, leading with the right hand on the left side of the horse, and proceed at the walk.

2. Halt; yield the haunches 180°.

3. Walk on; lateral yield to the right.

4. Halt, and switch the side you're leading from.

5. Halt; yield the haunches 180°, and then proceed at the walk.

6. Lateral yield to the left back to the track.

7. Switch the side you're leading from during the movement.

8. From the walk, yield the forehand 90° to the right.

9. Trot.

10. Walk.

11. From the walk, yield the forehand 90° to the right.

12. Lateral yield to the right to quarterline, then switch the side you're leading from.

13. Yield the haunches 180°.

14. Lateral yield to centerline.

15. Halt, and end the exercise.

FIGURES AND DIMENSIONS
— Lateral yields in steps 2, 6, 12, 15: about 5 meters (15 feet)

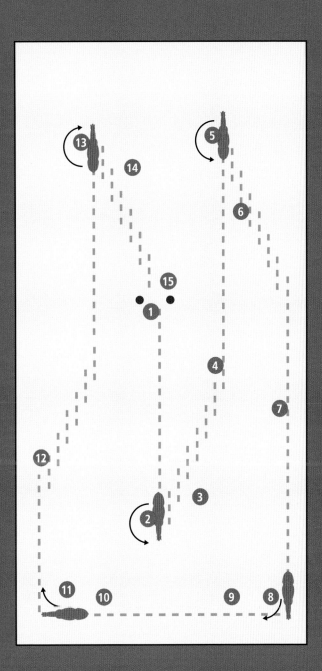

41

☞ EXERCISE 4: TROT VARIATIONS

This is a sample exercise for school figures in the trot.

1. Enter at a walk, leading with the right hand on the left side of the horse, and proceed at the walk.

2. Trot.

3. Volte to the right, 10 meters in diameter.

4. Transition to walk.

5. Change of rein at the walk, then trot.

6. Four-loop serpentine, with walk; switch the side you're leading from over the centerline.

7. Halt; rein-back one horse-length.

8. Trot, working trot.

9. Follow the short diagonal to the centerline, lengthening steps.

10. Halt, and end the exercise.

FIGURES AND DIMENSIONS
— Volte: 10 meters (33 feet) in diameter

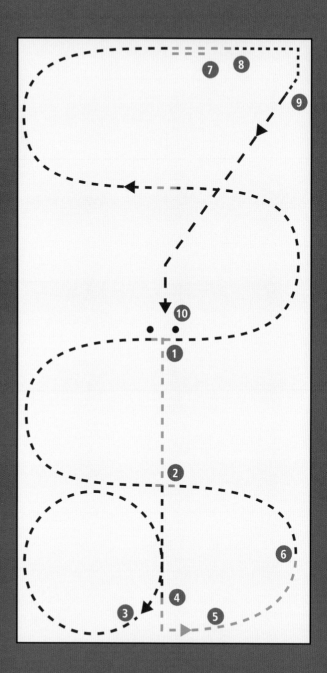

IN-HAND INSPECTION

In-hand inspection "on the triangle" is used as a tool to evaluate horses, and happens mostly at horse breed events. Here are some of the basics of presenting on the triangle, because it's a good exercise for any horse and handler.

The horse is presented in a bridle. The handler takes the reins about a foot below the bit, with the reins folded over one or two times in her right hand. Her index and middle fingers part the reins. The buckle at the end of the reins should be unbuckled. During the presentation, her right hand is carried calmly, slightly underneath the horse's head, with slack reins. Her left arm is held loose with a little bend, but should not swing back and forth, as that might confuse the horse.

ON THE TRIANGLE

The handler walks next to the horse to the starting point, which is usually about 7–14 feet away from where the judges—or, in your non-judged exercise, any observers—stand. The handler halts and takes a big step forward with her right leg, rotating and turning halfway on that foot. Then she stops about 2 feet

in front of the horse, facing him. The reins are now divided; her left hand takes the right rein, and her right hand takes the left rein. Her arms are bent and should be carried slightly underneath the horse's head without touching his head or obscuring it from view. The handler stands up straight, with positive tension through her body. The horse should stand in an open stance. At this point, the horse is viewed by the observers from the left side. The left front leg should be placed slightly ahead of the right front leg, and the left hind leg slightly behind the right hind leg. Later, at the final lineup, the open stance is reversed accordingly.

Next, the handler turns to face the observers and states her name, the name of the horse, the age of the horse, and possibly the lineage of the horse.

Then the handler makes a half turn back next to the horse's neck, takes the reins properly into her right hand, and proceeds on a straight line away from the starting point, toward the first turning marker.

At the marker, she should use the reins to guide the head of the horse into a slight right turn and proceed in walk to the next marker.

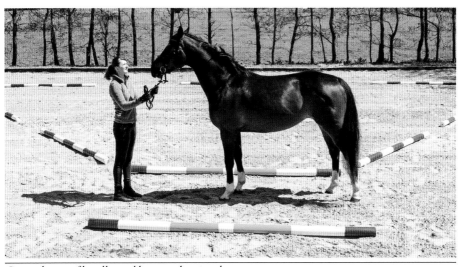

Correct lineup of handler and horse on the triangle.

At the second marker, the handler should lift her left hand to the height of the horse's head; this restricts the head and helps execute this turn. The horse and the handler then proceed in walk down the second leg of the triangle, returning to the starting point. Next, the handler can repeat the triangle at the trot, leading the horse to that first slight right turn, and using clucking sounds to alert the horse to the upcoming trot transition. She then straightens the horse in the direction of travel and transitions into a working trot in unison with the horse. Before the second turning marker, the horse

is asked to transition back to the walk and once again performs a small right turn as previously described, then proceeds down the second line and back toward the starting point in working trot.

Once the starting point is reached in trot, the horse is led past where he is presented and turned in a tight right turn at a marker placed about 10 meters (33 feet) beyond the starting point. Back at the starting point, the horse is presented from the right side for the final lineup. The whole presentation should be executed correctly, in unison and with almost invisible cues.

Walk along the left side of the triangle.

A transition from trot to walk on the trotted triangle.

Walk along the right side of the triangle.

Returning to the starting point.

Presentation of the right side of the body.

🖝 EXERCISE 5: CHUTES AND LADDERS

This is a sample exercise executed at the walk.

Enter at a walk, leading with the right hand on the left side of the horse.

1. Lead the horse through the chute of cones; track left; turn on the centerline.

2. Weave between the cones.

3-4. Change of rein along the short diagonal; increase your pace.

4-5. Walk with noticeably reduced pace.

5. Turn to the right.

6. Halt and switch the side you're leading from; walk off and track left.

7. Halt inside the chute of cones; walk off and then halt where you began, and end the exercise.

EQUIPMENT
— 15 cones

FIGURES AND DIMENSIONS
— Weaving section: cones 23 feet (7 meters) apart
— Slow walk: about 33 feet (10 meters)
— Cone chute: 5 feet (1.5 meters) wide

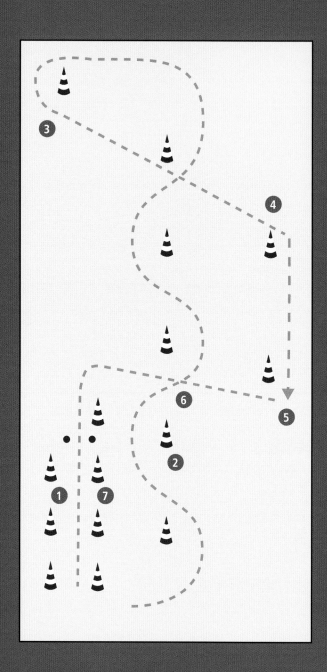

☞ EXERCISE 6: MERRY-GO-ROUND

This is a sample exercise executed in the walk and trot.

Enter at a walk, leading with the right hand on the left side of the horse.

1. Walk up the centerline; start in cone chute, and then volte right and volte left before continuing on the centerline, tracking left once you reach the short side of the arena.

2. Trot transition; trot to the end of the long side and transition back to walk.

3. Half circle and back to the track.

4. Switch the side you're leading from, proceeding at a collected walk.

5. Switch the side you're leading from again.

6 Enter the cone chute and halt at the end; rein-back for 4 steps, and then walk off. Halt and end the exercise.

EQUIPMENT
— 13 cones

FIGURES AND DIMENSIONS
— Volte: approx. 8–10 meters (26–33 feet)
— Collected walk: about 10 meters (33 feet)

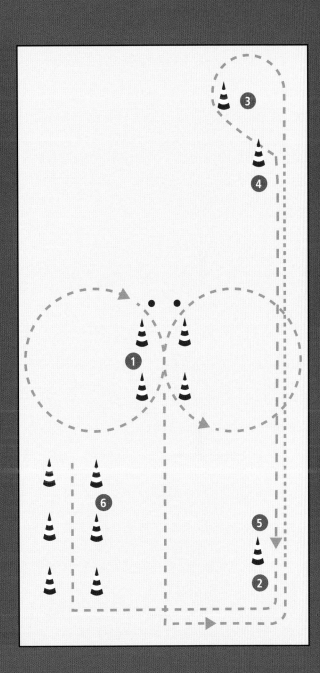

EXERCISE 7: TARP AND SLALOM 1

This is a sample exercise executed at the walk.

1. Enter at a walk, leading with the right hand on the left side of the horse.

2. Walk, tracking left, weaving through the cones on the long side.

3. Halt over the pole, and then walk off.

4. Proceed through the U-shaped maze of poles.

5. Change of rein across the long diagonal, and then lead the horse over the walk poles.

6. Walk across the tarp.

7. Halt and end the exercise.

EQUIPMENT

— 5 cones
— 1 tarp
— 3 ground poles for the walk pole section
— 1 ground pole for the halt
—11 ground poles for the U-shaped maze
— 30 ground pole anchors

FIGURES AND DIMENSIONS

— Weaving section: cones 23 feet (7 meters) apart
— U-shaped maze: sides 4–5 feet (1.2–1.5 meters) apart
— Walk poles: about 2½ feet (.8 meters) apart

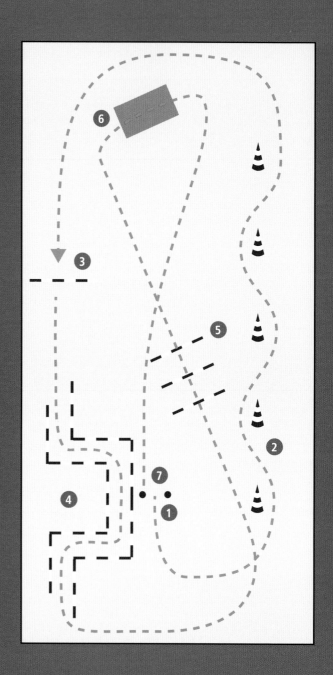

☞ EXERCISE 8: TARP AND SLALOM 2

This is a sample exercise executed at the walk.

1. Enter at a walk, leading with the right hand on the left side of the horse.

2. Walk, tracking right, weaving through the cones on the long side.

3. Halt over the pole, and then proceed at the walk.

4. Go through the double-U maze; change rein across the long diagonal.

5. Lead the horse over the walk poles.

6. Walk over the tarp.

7. Halt, and end the exercise.

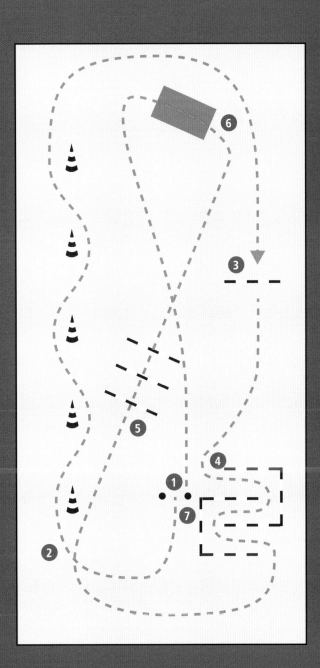

EQUIPMENT

— 5 cones
— 1 tarp
— 3 ground poles for the walk pole section
— 1 ground pole for the halt
— 6 ground poles for the double-U maze
— 20 ground pole anchors

FIGURES AND DIMENSIONS

— Weaving section: cones 23 feet (7 meters) apart
— Double-U maze: sides 4–5 feet (1.2–1.5 meters) apart
— Walk poles: about 2½ feet (.8 meters) apart

☞ EXERCISE 9: TRAPEZOID

This is a sample exercise executed at the walk.

1. Line up at the halt.

1–2. Proceed along the first side of the triangular track at the walk.

2–3. Trot to 3, and then transition to walk.

4. Line up, facing in the opposite direction from step 1, and then turn around and proceed at a walk to the short side.

5. Weave between the cones at the walk; at the corner (6), switch the side you're leading from.

6–7. Trot; at 7, transition back to walk.

7–8. Slow walk; at 8, switch the side you're leading from again.

9. Walk over the tarp.

10. Halt over the pole.

11. Proceed through the U-shaped maze.

12. Halt, and end the exercise.

EQUIPMENT
— 3 cones
— 1 tarp
— 10 ground poles to mark out a triangular track
— 2 ground poles for the halt
— 7 ground poles for the U-shaped maze
— 38 ground pole anchors

FIGURES AND DIMENSIONS
— U-shaped maze: sides 4–5 feet (1.2–1.5 meters) apart
— Poles: about 2½ feet (.8 meters) apart

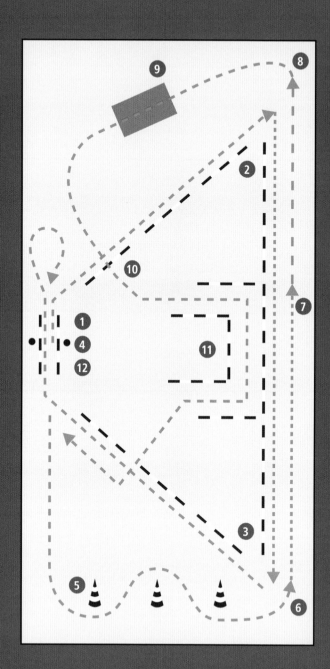

TRAINING OVER POLES

Training over poles improves the horse's agility and suppleness. The variety in the tasks required also encourages the horse's interest and willingness to cooperate, and promotes calmness and consistency. Your ability to lead him accurately must be advanced in order to complete different exercises over poles safely. Here, too, harmony and interaction between handler and horse are important. The application of your aids should be appropriate and unobtrusive.

A wooden anchor for ground poles, approx. 3–4 inches tall.

GROUND POLES

Work over ground poles is intended to improve the horse's sure-footedness and sense of balance. It also promotes a wider range of motion to encourage tracking up. Use anchors or stackers to prevent poles from rolling away.

During the warm-up phase, the handler must test the horse's control and ability to focus: experiment with various combinations of different tempos, halt, and rein-back, and with controlling individual steps. Then check the horse's reaction to a single pole. Only when his response is calm and composed should you move on to work with multiple poles and start constructing different kinds of obstacles with them:

— Pole chute (start with the poles 5 feet apart, and then reduce the distance to 3 feet)

— L-shape with poles

— Pole maze

— Simple U-shape with poles

— Double U-shape with poles

L-SHAPE WITH POLES

The simplest type of pole "maze" is an L-shape made with ground poles. It tests the precision of the aids as well as the agility of horse and handler.

The groove in the wood anchors the ground pole.

The distance between the ground poles should initially be wide, about 5 feet, and can later be reduced to around 3 feet, depending on the horse's level of experience. If the handler walks alongside the horse in the pole chute, its width should only be reduced to 4 feet. If the handler stays outside the chute, the width for horses can be reduced to 3 feet, and the width for ponies can come down to 2½ feet.

In turns that are the size of a volte (8–10 meters—26–32 feet), the horse should be supple, able to stay on the track and show good balance, before you attempt exercises with tighter turns (L-shaped or U-shaped pole mazes).

First, lead the horse into the chute at the walk. Before the turn, slow the pace noticeably, and proceed to lead one step at a time. To execute the turn, give the sideways cue at the moment when the horse's right front foot leaves the ground.

Leading the horse through a pole chute.

Leading through an L-shape, with bend.

Bend to the right in a double U-shape.

A left turn with good spacing.

Successful turns depend on precise, nuanced cues and correct timing. Turn your own body into the turn as well; your outside hip and shoulder should lead you into the turn. The horse must respond to your body language and cues. If he doesn't respond to a lateral cue with the halter or bit, direct his head by lifting your left hand.

After a few training sessions, the horse should be able to execute these exercises with proper bend and flexion, which will allow the hind feet to track up properly. Depending on the layout and width of the chute, the handler may be inside the chute or outside; either way, you are always beside the horse, and you should pick a consistent position (do not alternate between leading from inside the chute and leading from outside).

If the L-shape is practiced with a left turn in the L instead of a right turn, you should enter the chute at a walk and only slow the pace slightly—in this direction, the horse must make his turn on a bigger circle. The handler uses cues with her right arm to ensure that the horse walks on this bigger circle and doesn't follow in her footsteps instead.

The handler should walk holding her right hand slightly forward and turning her body to the left, causing her right shoulder and hip to point more ahead of her. With these cues from her body, the handler bends the horse to the left and sends him outward.

POLE MAZE

As your training progresses, more than one L-shape can be connected to create alternating turns to the right and left and make a maze.

As always, the intention of these obstacles is to encourage trusting interactions between human and horse, and the unobtrusive, skillful, and timely application of aids in the turns.

"OVER" OBSTACLES

— Halting over a pole.

— Crossing several poles at the walk (with the poles about 2½ feet apart) or trot (with the poles about 4 feet apart), slowly increasing the number of poles.

— Crossing irregular rows of poles.

— Moving over a round pole cross.

— Moving over a ground pole fan.

First, lead the horse calmly toward the poles and note whether the horse walks confidently, without clipping the poles, as he moves through the obstacles. Alternate which side you're leading from. Ideally, the horse should adjust the bend through his body evenly to match the bend of the given line of travel. You must ensure that you stay in the right position relative to the horse, with your lead hand next to him. At first, stay inside the pole chute or maze. Add difficulty by leading the horse from outside the poles, or by asking for a rein-back inside the obstacle.

It's important for the horse to cross the poles calmly but attentively. He must not decide to just jump everything—if he does, that is a clear sign of tension and could be dangerous for the handler.

When working with poles, it's important not to repeat any given exercise too often. Try an exercise three to five times at the most. It's better to praise the horse and move on after one well-executed attempt than to request the same thing too many times.

HALTING OVER POLES

Work up to halting over a pole in small stages.

— The pole should be secured to prevent it from rolling.

— The horse should halt reliably and be able to respond correctly to cues for individual forward steps as well as cues for half steps.

— The horse should not be afraid to step calmly over a pole.

At first, lead the horse at a calm walk over the pole. Then, ask him to halt in front of the pole and after crossing the pole. Next, ask him to halt directly in front of the pole, and from there, lead him slowly over the pole. Only if the horse remains relaxed at this point in the exercise can you start to ask him to halt over the pole.

Both handler and horse show efficient and focused push-off over poles of varying heights.

Breathe and count to five: An accomplished and square halt over the pole.

With a solid foundation for the exercise, the horse is led perfectly straight.

Simultaneous lifting of the legs of horse and handler.

Come to a halt directly in front of the pole; give a cue with your voice, the halter, and your body language to initiate a half-step forward, and then catch the step before it is completed, coming back to the halt. Give lots of praise if the horse's front feet landed in front of the pole and his hind feet remained behind the pole. Then lead him in a calm walk.

You can refine your approach further still by leading the horse toward the pole at the walk, and then, about one horse-length in front of the pole, reducing the pace until you ask the horse to halt over the pole.

IRREGULAR ROW OF POLES

Horses must first be able to step over a single pole reliably and calmly before you gradually add more poles.

The handler should be positioned half an arm's length from the horse, at his side. The horse is then brought toward the first pole in a calm working walk. He should step over the pole with confidence and move in a straight line.

This exercise requires focus from both human and horse, as the poles are placed at different heights and the handler's and horse's steps must be adjusted accordingly.

Four to six poles should be placed with one end at a height of about 6–10 inches on a riser; alternate which end of the pole is raised from one pole to the next.

At the walk, the distance between the poles should be 2½–3 feet for horses and, depending on their size, 2–2½ feet for ponies. Horse and handler teams that are more experienced can work over irregular poles at the trot, with the poles placed about 4 feet apart (or, for ponies, about 3 feet apart).

MULTI-SIDED POLE CROSS

The pole cross offers an even higher level of difficulty than the irregular. In this exercise, four poles, each 10–13 feet long, are placed in a square. One end of each pole is resting on top of the next pole over in one direction, while the other end is resting underneath the next pole over in the other direction.

This arrangement links the poles together well and prevents them from rolling away easily. The poles should overlap at the corners by about 20 inches, resulting in a cross pattern.

Success in this exercise depends on the agility of the horse on the one hand, and on the precision of the handler on the other. The handler must lead the horse in a straight line over the crossed poles in one corner, into the square, and then diagonally out over the crossed poles in the opposite corner. Assessing the varying heights of the intersecting poles accurately adds yet another challenge for the handler and the horse.

Work in small, consecutive stages to master this exercise.

— Enter over one of the long straight sides of the square into the obstacle, walk straight across, and exit at the opposite long side.

— Move the poles at one corner far enough apart to allow you to lead the horse into the square through the resulting gap and get back out over a long side.

— Walk into the square through the gap between the poles in one corner, and straight ahead back out over the crossed poles of the opposite corner.

— Enter over a long side of the square, turn inside the square, and exit over the crossed poles in one corner.

— Enter over one crossed corner of the square and, coming across the diagonal, exit over the crossed corner on the opposite side.

If difficulties arise, the handler should be able to assess the situation correctly and come up with a variety of options to solve the problem. This includes asking less of the horse. If necessary, more training steps can be added in between those outlined above, or previous exercises can be repeated to restore the horse's confidence.

POLE FAN

To create a pole fan, position several ground poles so that one end is raised and set into the cup on a jumping standard, and the other end is on the ground. The distances between the ends of the poles on the ground should be even, and appropriate for the gait and the size of the horse. This obstacle requires focus from both the handler and the horse when stepping over the poles, as the angle of the incline causes each pole to present a different height to each foot.

Exact aim over the crossed poles in the corners.

Moving through the pole square with good focus.

55

The turn to the left here is still tentative.

The turn to the right in the pole fan is not a problem ...

... and is also smoothly executed at the trot.

REIN-BACK IN AN OBSTACLE

Another step in the education of the horse is the rein-back in or between obstacles or surrounding objects. For insecure horses, it's initially easier to back up in an open space rather than in a restricted space between objects. They tend to want to sidestep or swerve to get a look at the blind spot directly behind them. For this reason, using subtle cues, you should first work on a straight, smooth rein-back. Horses only back up willingly between objects or on uneven ground when their confidence in themselves and their handler is established.

Simply walk through the chute of poles first, and work on halting calmly at different points inside and outside the chute.

Then add single steps backwards—first out of the chute, and then inside the chute. Only after that exercise is established should you start working on backing into the chute.

The horse must have previously learned to take individual steps backwards easily and willingly. He must also know to pause when prompted, so you can help him avoid bumping into poles or objects that are located in the blind spot behind him, and therefore he will not lose his confidence in your abilities as his handler. This same strategy can be employed as you work on other obstacles.

BACKING INTO TURNS

The next level of difficulty consists of backing into turns, as for weaving between cones, in an L-shape or in a maze in different variations, as well as backing into other kinds of obstacles like a tarp, umbrellas, ribbons, or similar objects. The prerequisite here is that you are readily able to control the horse during every step forward, backward, and sideways. Switch the side you're leading from when backing into turns as necessary—you should be on whichever side needs a cue applied. You must be able to manage the horse's sideway steps with subtle cues to avoid having him bump into obstacles.

... sideways around the corner.

First, back up straight all the way to the corner ...

Then center the horse between the poles ...

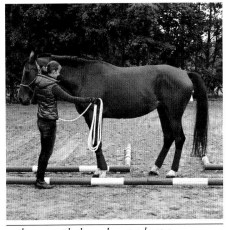

... then move the haunches, step by step ...

... and back him straight into a halt.

57

BOTTLENECKS

To lead or send a horse through bottlenecks like chutes of cones, poles, or barrels calls for a keen ability to influence and direct the horse efficiently. The intended line of movement must be maintained reliably and at a relaxed pace.

It's mostly the human handler who needs to learn to apply suitable forward driving aids and to stay calm during work on bottlenecks like these. Driving aids that are too strong or too hasty cause the horse to avoid the obstacle, or even to turn and run away.

The ability to "read" the horse, to interpret his state of mind accurately, plays an important role in the success of these exercises: is the horse curious, playful, brave, uncertain, scared, or in a state of panic?

It's not possible to achieve lasting success with challenging work like familiarizing the horse with objects he finds frightening without the ability to assess him accurately.

Slowing the pace before the bottleneck, then stepping thro front of the horse.

At first, Bärchen the pony looks skeptical, and Maja gives him time.

Both pony and handler pass under the pole together, which promotes confidence.

☞ EXERCISE 10: FOR YOUNG HORSES

This is a sample exercise that is well suited to young horses.

1. Enter at the walk.

2. Proceed at a walk; when you reach the short side, track right.

3. Weave between the cones.

4. Halt and switch the side you're leading from.

5. Lead the horse through a figure eight; at the point of intersection, switch the side you're leading from again.

6. Trot.

7. Transition to walk; maintain a slow walk to the middle of the short side.

8. Halt.

9. Rein-back for 6 steps.

10. Change rein across the long diagonal.

11. Lead the horse across one pole.

12. Lead the horse across three walk poles.

13. Turn on the centerline, halt, and end the exercise.

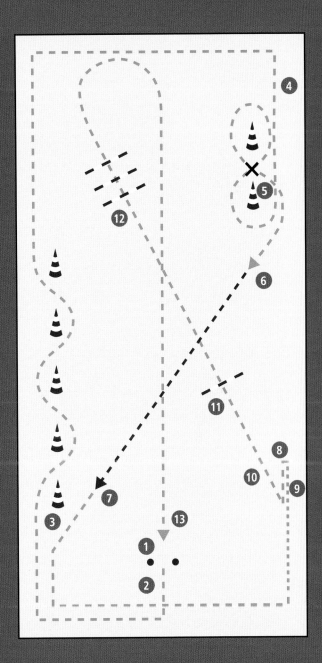

EQUIPMENT
— 7 cones
— 4 ground poles, 10 feet (3 meters) long
— 8 pole anchors

FIGURES AND DIMENSIONS
— Weaving section: cones 23 feet (7 meters) apart
— Volte: 8 meters (26 feet) in diameter
— Walk poles: about 2½–3 feet (.8–.9 meters) apart

☞ EXERCISE 11: TAKE IT UP A NOTCH

This is a sample exercise for young horses that is more advanced, done in walk and trot.

1. Enter at a walk, leading with the right hand on the left side of the horse; halt on the centerline. Proceed at walk; when you reach the short side, track left.

2. Halt in the pole chute; stand still for 5 seconds, and then proceed at the walk.

3. Weave between the cones.

4. Trot.

5. Transition to walk.

6. Halt and switch the side you're leading from. Yield the haunches 180° to the left, and then proceed at walk.

7. Turn around, to the right.

8. Halt and rein-back for 4 steps; halt and switch the side you're leading from again; yield the haunches 90° to the right, and then proceed at walk.

9. Lead in a half circle toward the mounting block and halt; the handler steps on the mounting block, with the horse standing still for 5 seconds.

10. Turn on the centerline, halt, and end the exercise.

EQUIPMENT
— 5 cones
— 2 ground poles, 10 feet (3 meters) long
— 4 pole anchors
— 1 mounting block

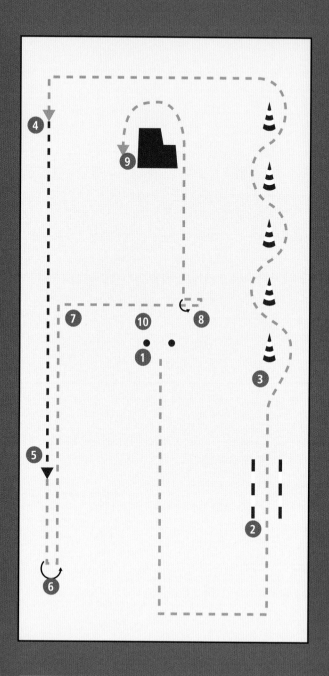

FIGURES AND DIMENSIONS
— Weaving section: cones 23 feet (7 meters) apart
— Ground poles: 5 feet (1.5 meters) apart

☞ EXERCISE 12: LEG DAY

1. Enter at a walk, leading with the right hand on the left side of the horse. Halt on the centerline, and then proceed at the walk; when you reach the short side, track right.

2. Lead the horse over the raised cavalletti.

3. Halt over the ground pole, with the horse standing still for 5 seconds.

4. Lead the horse over the three ground poles, then maintain a slow walk until making a right turn before the track; transition to medium walk.

5. Lead the horse over the pole fan.

6. Lead the horse over a row of poles of varying heights.

7. Trot.

8. Transition to walk.

9. Lead the horse over the pole cross lengthwise.

10. Perform a half circle and go back over the corners of the pole cross.

11. Return to the starting point, halt, and end the exercise.

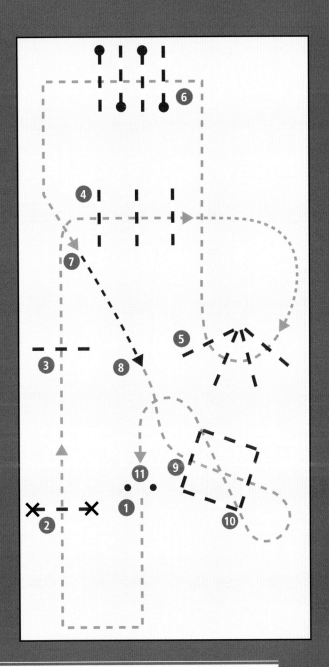

EQUIPMENT
— 1 cavalletti
— 4 cavalletti blocks
— 4 ground poles, 10–13 feet (3–4 meters) long
— 24 pole anchors

FIGURES AND DIMENSIONS
— Cavalletti height: about ½ foot (20 cm)
— Ground poles: 6 feet (1.8 meters) apart
— Uneven row: poles 2½ feet (.8 meters) apart
— Ends of poles in fan, around the outside: about 3 feet (.9 meters) apart
— Overlap in the corners of the pole cross: 1½ feet (.5 meters)

☞ EXERCISE 13: DEVELOPING BEND

This is a sample exercise that focuses on "developing bend" in the walk and trot.

1. Enter at a walk, leading with the right hand on the left side of the horse, and halt on the centerline. Proceed at the walk; when you reach the short side, track left.

2. Lead the horse through the L-shape.

3. Lead the horse through the second L-shape.

4. Change rein across the long diagonal, weaving between the cones there and then back.

5. Lead the horse back through the pole corner from step 2.

6. Halt and switch the side you're leading from; proceed at the walk.

7. Lead the horse through the combined U-shapes maze.

8. Trot.

9. Volte to the right, one and a quarter times around.

10. Transition to walk; "S" change of rein through volte.

11. Switch the side you're leading from again in the center of the volte.

12. Trot; volte to the left at the trot.

13. Transition back to walk.

14. Lead the horse through the cone "gates."

15. Halt, and end the exercise.

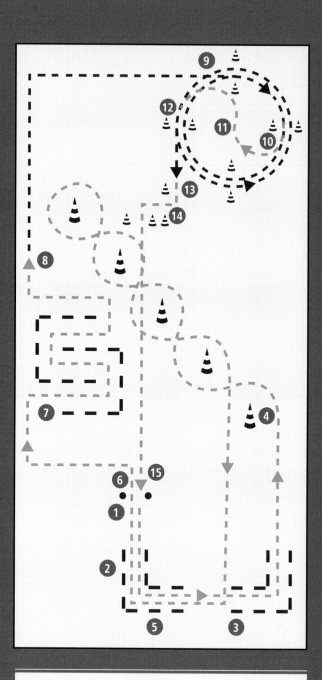

EQUIPMENT
— 17 cones
— 14 ground poles, 10 feet (3 meters) long
— 28 pole anchors

FIGURES AND DIMENSIONS
---- Weaving section: cones 23 feet (7 meters) apart
---- Cone gates: 4–5 feet (1.2–1.5 meters) apart
---- Pole corner: poles 4 feet (1.2 meters) apart
---- Double-U maze: poles 4–5 feet (1.2–1.5 meters) apart

THOUGHTFUL DESENSITIZATION

Since horses are flight animals by nature, their tendency to spook, as well as the training to avoid creating dangerous situations for you and for them, requires special considerations. This involves both correct behavior from humans as well as thoughtful desensitization of the horse. This training consists of recreating various everyday situations in order to work on establishing confident responses and behaviors. The horse learns to trust the handler and not feel like he must run from every unknown object. His innate curiosity is integrated into the learning process. He should approach scary obstacles independently, in a composed manner. He should look at it and assess it as "harmless."

Easygoing horses have learned to trust humans, and so they live with less anxiety and more inner calm. Success with this kind of training can never be achieved with aids that are too intense, too rough, or too controlling. Training sessions should initially take place in the arena, or in a secure, fenced-in area to prevent injuries to the horse—or to others, should a horse panic.

A tarp in the wind is very scary for horses.

Horse and handler must have established good foundations during earlier training sessions with groundwork, and must have a confident grasp of skills like tempo control, halting, leading on bending lines, and changing which side the handler is leading from. They should rehearse these exercises again in preparation for desensitization training. The horse should be comfortable walking next to the handler attentively, on a slack but not loose rein.

The handler should always walk between any "scary obstacle" and the horse; if the horse panics, he will move away from the obstacle, and thus away from the handler, which allows her to avoid injury.

Such calm—despite the flapping tarp—is a wonderful success.

The horse is always going to try to avoid the object. Make sure you stay out of his flight path by either changing the side you are leading him from or choosing the direction you both approach the object from accordingly.

COMPOSURE

Obstacles can be used to check how willing the horse is to accept an object, and to familiarize him with them so he no longer feels any need to panic.

Some of these obstacles, like the tarp or the bridge, allow you to lead the horse from a distance, but you must have some experience in leading from that position instead of from beside the horse. When working on overcoming a tarp or a bridge in particular, the horse might initially react spontaneously and erratically; he might swerve and back up, or turn away from the obstacle. In that situation, the handler must maintain her composure and react appropriately. Keep the "four Fs" (Flight, Fight, Freeze, and an additional option, Flirt, all outlined in the next section).

Horses should learn to respond to their surroundings with confidence and composure. It takes a horse time to assess an object he isn't familiar with, during which he may want to wait to see whether it develops a life of its own (like a hidden predator in nature, who might also wait quietly at first and then abruptly move). During that wait, horses are usually visibly tense and will be ready for flight at a moment's notice. If the handler doesn't allow the horse to have this time, but instead tries to rush this assessment phase by pushing the horse toward the object with driving aids, she might provoke more serious resistance in the horse. We tend to label a horse stubborn when he has given up on active resistance but is still not willing to move forward. However, that's just normal horse behavior when trying to avoid a situation that seems potentially dangerous. It will take a moment before the horse will show renewed interest in the "scary" object. Solid instruction and experience are needed to correctly judge the horse's behavior.

FLIGHT RESPONSES

The release of adrenaline prepares a horse's body for imminent flight in potentially dangerous situations, and the decision to flee is usually made spontaneously and very abruptly. Only after the horse has put some distance between himself and the "scary" object will he stop and re-evaluate the situation. With some practice, it's possible to recognize the signs a horse displays right before he takes flight. The horse lifts his head; his ears are pricked in one direction, his body is tense, and his back is tight. In dangerous situations, horses display a specific, predictable pattern of possible responses.

Flight: Running away, jumping sideways, stopping suddenly and dodging, hastily backing up.

Fight: If flight is not an option (the horse is in a small space or tied up), lashing out with front or back legs, biting, rearing.

Freeze: In the instant the horse becomes aware of a possible danger, a "freeze" response means a high neck position and a rigid head posture, both of which signal a high likelihood of flight as the next response. As a reaction and after a fight response has proven ineffective, a freeze response means the horse is abruptly unmoving, seemingly apathetic, with rigid body posture, and shows no reaction when addressed with voice or touch. The horse has withdrawn completely.

Flirt: An additional option that usually shows up as small attempts to break free from a "freeze" state and explore ways out of the situation. The horse's responses may include looking at the object, blinking, approaching the object with small steps, snorting, stretching his head and neck slowly towards the object, touching it with his nose and examining it, using a foot to tap the ground or the object, and exploring by pawing.

Creating noise with a barrel.

Playing polo with a broom and a large ball.

Rolling the ball down a chute of cones.

Parking at the mounting block.

Training with the squeeze bottle.

Leading across a hose.

Bravely sniffing the umbrella. *Then it's possible to pass close beside it.*

"RATTLE SACK"

With the help of a "rattle sack," the horse can learn that even unknown sounds and noises can be tolerated and taken in with a calm demeanor. Any kind of canvas sack that can be filled with empty cans or similar items is suitable as a "rattle sack," and pulled with a rope.

First, the horse should be allowed to inspect the rattle sack. Depending on how curious he is, this may initially be a careful inspection but then increase in intensity.

Some horses even try to paw at the sack with a foot to explore it more thoroughly. If the horse is more dubious, it's fine to allow this kind of exploration, but you should let the horse stop and move away, too. For brief moments at a time, a helper should then move the sack back and forth in front of the horse. If the horse remains calm, the helper can move in a bigger arc around the horse. This can be followed by circling the standing horse with the rattle sack, while maintaining a long distance.

Once the horse is ready to walk, a helper can first pull the rattle sack alongside the horse's shoulder at a safe distance (at least 13 feet / 4 meters), then move to walk ahead of the horse while pulling the sack along. As

the horse's acceptance of the rattle sack increases, the rattle sack can be allowed to fall farther behind the horse, where he can't see it as well. With that accomplished, it should soon be possible to suddenly pull on the rattle sack while the horse is right next to the helper who's doing the pulling. This method of gradually increasing exposure also applies to other obstacles.

RIBBON CURTAIN

The horse must be able to deal with a visual stimulus that is placed above him and will touch his body as he walks through it. Once again, it's important to work up to this obstacle in small increments in order to build the trust and confidence of the horse.

The ribbon curtain should be hung around 7½ feet off the ground, and should be 8–10 feet wide. The ribbon bands should hang to about 1½ feet above the ground. The structure suspending the curtain must be set up securely enough to prevent it from falling over.

Start by leading the horse past the ribbon curtain at some distance away from it, with the handler walking between the curtain and

The jacket hanging over the fence "was not there earlier."

the horse. If the horse remains calm, approach the ribbon curtain and let the horse inspect it.

Then, part the curtain to create a big opening and slowly lead the horse through. If the horse continues to remain calm and relaxed, decrease the size of the opening bit by bit until the curtain hangs in its original state. The horse must already be familiar with touches on both his left and right sides.

UMBRELLA, BALL, AND FRIENDS

As with previous objects, obstacles like umbrellas, balls, rattle sacks or rattle carts, balloons, ribbon curtains, and more are introduced to the horse slowly and worked on in small increments. The horse should show interest in the objects but remain mentally "with" the handler.

With the umbrella, start by opening it and setting it on the ground. The horse should initially look at and sniff it. As soon as that is possible without a fearful reaction, the horse should then be calmly walked past the umbrella, with the handler always staying between the umbrella and the horse.

Repeatedly stopping and praising the horse offers him reassurance.

The same exercise should be repeated while tracking the opposite way and leading from the opposite side. If the horse shows no evasive reactions, a second person can pick up and hold the umbrella. The horse is made familiar with this new situation in the same way as previously described. After a few of these practice sessions, it becomes possible to work on opening and closing the umbrella in the presence of the horse.

First, the closed umbrella should be presented to the horse. If the horse no longer tries to avoid it but instead shows curiosity, let him touch and investigate the umbrella repeatedly. It is important for the intensity of this stimulation to remain below the horse's threshold for flight.

Then the umbrella should be slowly opened, partially and then fully, in front of the horse. As soon as the horse shows any signs of startlement or distress, begin re-closing the umbrella—reduce the amount of stimulus you are asking him to tolerate—and only start opening it again once the horse's trust and confidence are coming back.

Horses should also not easily be startled by visual obstacles that are coming toward them; in the real world, this could mean cars or bicycles, but for these exercises, balls are good preparation. Your horse should already have a solid foundation of successful groundwork exercises before you start working on this.

Once the horse is led around a ball, he should be allowed to look at the ball and touch it with his nose. The ball will then be rolled away from the horse, and the horse led along, following it (so the horse is chasing the ball, rather than the ball chasing the horse). After that, the ball can be slowly rolled toward the horse while he stands at a halt. He should remain halted, with a composed, inquisitive, and relaxed demeanor.

First, the horse inspects the tarp with his neck long, but ...

... he remains doubtful when stepping on it. Once again ..

TARP ON THE GROUND

Taking small steps, the horse will probably approach the tarp with both curiosity and caution. You can fold the tarp into a narrow strip to make it smaller and less frightening at first. When the horse lowers his head and neck to inspect the tarp, sniffing and snorting with his nose, it is important to let him do it.

He'll likely paw the tarp with one foot, trying to check the surface. Only then will he gingerly try to step on it or walk across it. However, some horses may decide to start with a big jump instead—so the handler should stand at a safe distance from the horse and watch him closely. With growing confidence after multiple tries, the horse will walk more and more calmly across the tarp. He'll reach the point where a change in the tarp's position won't bother him, either.

When working on crossing the tarp, the handler should walk back and forth across the tarp first, to get the horse used to the sound it makes. Then, she should lead the horse to and around a narrow strip of tarp. During this process, the handler should always remain between the horse and the tarp to avoid being pushed by the horse if he gets nervous and wants to move away from the tarp.

.... trust allows him to cross the tarp despite his doubts.

Whether you are leading at close range or from a distance, the horse must still be allowed time to examine the tarp with his nose and feet by sniffing and pawing. Once the horse appears calm and composed, lead him across the tarp. Gradually, the tarp can be unfolded to its full size, while you continue to monitor the horse's reaction. Once the horse is comfortable with the full tarp, you can also try moving the tarp to a new practice area.

The quality of your tarp matters. It should be firm and durable to prevent tearing when the horse paws at it with his feet. It should also be secured around the edges with sand or poles to keep it from blowing in the wind.

☞ EXERCISE 14: SOME OF EVERYTHING

This is a sample exercise with "some of everything," in the walk and trot.

1. Enter at a walk, leading with the right hand on the left side of the horse, and halt on the centerline. Proceed at the walk; when you reach the short side, track right.

2. Trot.

3. Transition back to walk.

4. Walk through the bottleneck/pole chute.

5. Lead the horse past three open umbrellas.

6. Halt over the ground pole, and then walk on.

7. Halt.

8. Rein-back on a curve to the next two cones until the horse's front legs are between them; then proceed forward at the walk, and turn left.

9. Switch the side you're leading from during the walk.

10. Volte, 8 meters (26 feet) in diameter.

11. Lead the horse across a bridge or a tarp; continue to the short side and turn onto the centerline.

12. Trot.

13. Halt and end the exercise.

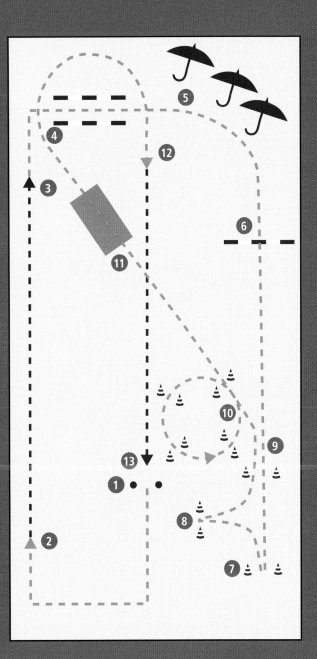

EQUIPMENT
— 14 cones
— 3 ground poles, 10 feet (3 meters) long
— 6 pole anchors
— 1 tarp or bridge
— 3 umbrellas

FIGURES AND DIMENSIONS
— Rein-back section: cones 4 feet (1.2 meters) apart, with sets of 2 positioned at right angles to each other about 10 feet (3 meters) apart
— Pole chute: poles 2½ feet (.8 meters) apart

☞ EXERCISE 15: LITTLE HORROR SHOW

This is a versatile sample exercise with many small "horror shows," executed at the walk.

1. Enter at the walk, leading with the right hand on the left side of the horse, and halt between the quarterline and the centerline. Proceed at the walk; when you reach the short side, track left.

2. Volte around an open umbrella lying on the ground, or a beach umbrella that is standing up.

3. Switch the side you're leading from in the walk.

4. Walk past umbrellas lying on the ground; have a helper holding one, opening and closing it (slowly!).

5. Kick the balls into the hula hoop.

6. Switch the side you're leading from again in the walk.

7. Lead the horse across a tarp.

8. Walk through a ribbon curtain.

9. Halt; use the spray bottle, applying 1–2 spritzes of water to each side of the horse's neck.

10. Halt; dribble the ball on the ground 5 times.

11. Halt; bang on the pot.

12. Return to the starting point, halt, and end the exercise.

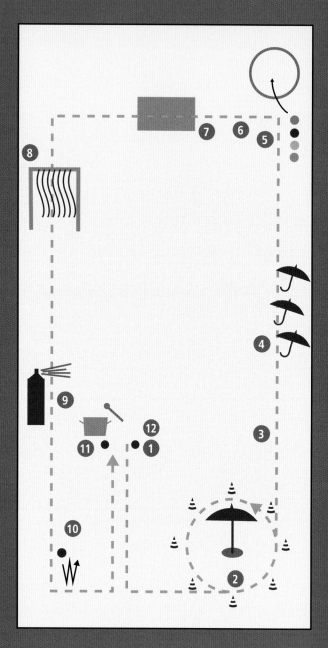

EQUIPMENT

— 4 umbrellas (or 3 regular umbrellas and 1 beach umbrella)
— 8 cones
— 1 tarp
— 5 balls
— 1 hula hoop
— 1 ribbon curtain
— 1 spray bottle of water
— 1 pot and wooden spoon

FIGURES AND DIMENSIONS

— Volte around open/standing umbrella: 8 meters (26 feet) in diameter
— Distance between obstacles and outside fence/wall: 5 feet (1.5 meters)

☞ EXERCISE 16: COMPOSURE TEST 1

This is a versatile sample exercise to test your horse's composure.

1. Enter at the walk, leading with the right hand on the left side of the horse, and halt on the centerline. Proceed at the trot, on the centerline.

2. Halt; proceed at the walk, and then track right.

3. Pick up the spray bottle, and apply 2 spritzes of water to each side of the horse's neck; proceed at the walk.

4. Halt; drape the tarp over the horse's back and have him remain standing still with it there for 5 seconds. Remove the tarp, and proceed at the walk.

5. Pass through the pool noodle gate.

6. Halt, bang on the pot (at least 3 times), and then proceed at the walk.

7. Lead the horse across the diagonal corners of the pole cross.

8. Lead the horse to the umbrella. Pick it up, open and close it 2 times, and then set it back down. Proceed at the walk, and turn up the centerline.

9. Trot.

10. Transition to collected walk.

11. Return to the starting point, halt, and end the exercise.

EQUIPMENT
— 1 spray bottle of water
— 1 tarp, at least 6½ x 10 feet (2 x 3 meters)
— 8 pool noodles
— 1 pot and wooden spoon
— 4 ground poles, anywhere from 6½–13 feet (2–4 meters) long
— 1 umbrella

FIGURES AND DIMENSIONS
— Overlap in corners of pole square: about 1½ feet (.5 meters)

☞ EXERCISE 17: COMPOSURE TEST 2

This is another possible sample exercise to test your horse's composure.

1. Enter at the walk, and halt at the end of the pole chute; then proceed at the walk.

2. Trot.

3. Transition back to walk.

4. Turn right around the cone.

5. Trot.

6. Transition back to walk.

7. In the pole chute, halt and switch the side you're leading from.

8. Lead the horse past 3 open umbrellas.

9. With a pole set up on some jump standards, and a blanket or tarp draped over the pole to "conceal" the balls at first, have a helper roll at least 3 balls out from under the tarp and toward you and the horse as you pass.

10. Lead the horse over the tarp.

11. Halt. Pick up the spray bottle and apply at least 3 spritzes of water to each side of the horse's neck, then switch the side you're leading from.

12. Roll the big ball out of the first square, then kick it into the second square.

13. Lead the horse through the cone chute; halt about 13 feet (4 meters) beyond the chute, at the cone.

14. Rein-back into the cone chute, and then walk forward to the rope gate.

15. Open the rope gate, walk through the gate, and close the gate (do not let the rope touch the ground).

16. Halt with the horse in the square of cones and the handler standing beside it, and end the exercise.

EQUIPMENT
— 12 cones
— 3 umbrellas
— 1 tarp/bridge
— 1 spray bottle of water
— Ball squares: 8 ground poles about 6½ feet (2 meters) long and 1 big ball
— Pole chute: 2 ground poles at least 10 feet (3 meters) long and 4 pole anchors
— Rope gate: 2 stable jumping standards and 1 thick rope about 10–13 feet (3–4 meters) long

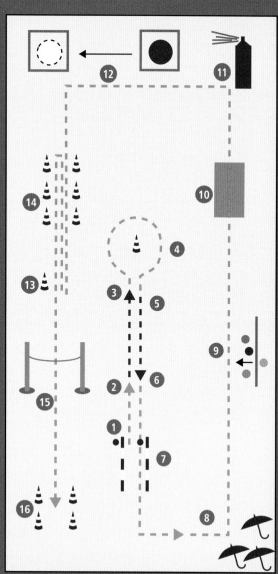

GROUNDWORK FOR CHILDREN

Groundwork exposes children to a variety of experiences with their ponies. To develop confidence, they will need a well-behaved, appropriately sized pony.

In the beginning, children tend to be either a little hesitant or completely unafraid when handling ponies. In both cases, they need solid instructions and easy beginner tasks. They should learn how ponies respond to cues and aids applied by a human. The exercises described on the following pages are meant to help develop both the child's own skills and their relationship with their pony. The pony shouldn't be managing the tasks on his own. Ideally, the pony will be sensitive enough to react to hesitant, unclear instructions with inaccuracy, which will teach the child to be clearer and more subtle with her body language and her cues. Children also often lack spatial awareness, which these exercises can help to improve and develop. In addition, they can't focus on a single task for as long as adolescents or adults can. For that reason, a variety of different exercises is a good idea.

When children feel safe, they become curious, and they tend to like to try out new things. Groundwork is a good tool to channel children's creativity and ensure the needs and behaviors of the horse are attended to. Usually, children aren't perceived as threats by horses and ponies, and they react honestly and directly, in the moment, just like horses. Horses' social instincts tend to respond to this similarity, and they often "watch out" for children and are careful when moving around them.

Even in situations that might normally startle or frighten horses, they often react with more composure when they are handled by children. But do not take this for granted. Children should learn right from the beginning how to handle a horse properly, and they

Maja and Bärchen are a well-rehearsed team. Walking through the double U-shape requires focus, timing, and the ability to remain calm.

need to be guided toward more difficult tasks one step at a time. As part of this learning process, children should develop mindfulness and become aware of stimuli that might affect the horse or pony. These things must be taught in a way that is age-appropriate for the child. Groundwork exercises are a helpful tool to introduce children to the idea of desensitization while working on different obstacles.

Children must learn that horses have their own way of perceiving the world around them and that they have their own specific needs, but that they are, at the same time, also clever, tender, and—with a good foundation of trust—very cooperative.

Weaving through a row of cones.

Crossing a tarp.

Rolling a ball between ground poles.

Placing a dowel into a cone.

Balancing on a beam.

Passing through a flapping ribbon curtain.

EXERCISE 18: WITH LEAD REIN AND CHILD MOUNTED

1. Enter at a walk, and halt.

2. Proceed at the walk; turn onto the second track.

3. Pick up a cup from a barrel.

4. Place the cup onto another barrel.

5. Weave between the cones.

6. Cross under a pool noodle resting on two jump standards (about 5 feet / 1.5 meters high).

7. Throw two balls into a bucket.

8. Walk across a row of uneven poles.

9. Pick up a cup from a barrel.

10. Proceed at the walk with the cup in hand to the next barrel; halt and place the cup on the barrel; pick up a second cup.

11. Place this second cup on a third barrel.

12. Roll a ball sitting on top of two poles with your hand.

13. Halt at the end of the poles and throw the ball into the bucket.

14. Walk back to the starting point, halt, and end the exercise.

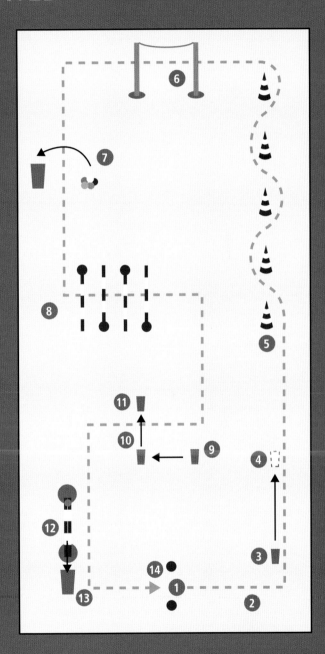

EQUIPMENT
— 5 cones
— 5 ground poles or 5 cavalletti
— 1 pool noodle
— 2 poles
— 5 barrels and 4 plastic cups
— 3 balls
— 2 buckets
— 2 jump standards

FIGURES AND DIMENSIONS
— Weaving section: cones 19–23 feet (6–7 meters) apart
— Uneven row: poles about 2 feet (.6–.7 meters) apart

☞ EXERCISE 19: PARTNER TRAIL

This is a sample exercise that can be done by 2 horse-handler teams at the same time.

1. Enter at a walk, next to each other. Halt at X.

2. Proceed at the walk on the centerline.

3. Split: one team should turn left and the other right.

4. Change of rein on each short diagonal respectively.

5. Switch the side you're leading from.

6. Halt and yield the haunches 180° to the outside.

7. Switch the side you're leading from again.

8. Walk to the cone, then transition to trot.

9. Halt, and yield the forehand 180° (a turn-on-the-haunches).

10. Proceed at the walk.

11. Weave between the cones.

12. Halt inside the pole chute.

13. Rein-back for 6 steps, then proceed at the walk.

14. Turn up the centerline.

15. Halt at X, and end the exercise.

EQUIPMENT
— 10 cones
— 4 ground poles, at least 10 feet (3 meters) long
— 8 pole anchors

FIGURES AND DIMENSIONS
— Weaving section: cones 23 feet (7 meters) apart
— Pole chute: poles 5 feet (1.5 meters) apart

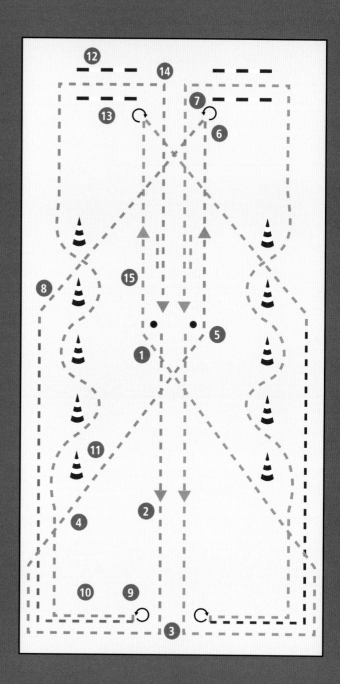

☞ EXERCISE 20: HANDLER AGILITY

This is a sample exercise that highlights the handler's agility.

1. Enter at a walk, halt, and then proceed at the walk.

2. Switch the side you're leading from in the walk.

3. Step across five uneven ground poles.

4. Roll the ball through the pole chute with a broom.

5. Switch the side you're leading from again in the walk.

6. Open the gate, walk through it, and close it.

7. Walk across the balance beam without touching the ground.

8. Return to the starting point, halt, and end the exercise.

EQUIPMENT
— 7 ground poles, at least 10 feet (3 meters) long
— 10 pole anchors
— 1 ball
— 1 broom
— 1 gate
— 1 sturdy balance beam

FIGURES AND DIMENSIONS
— Uneven row: poles about 2 feet (.8–.9 meters) apart

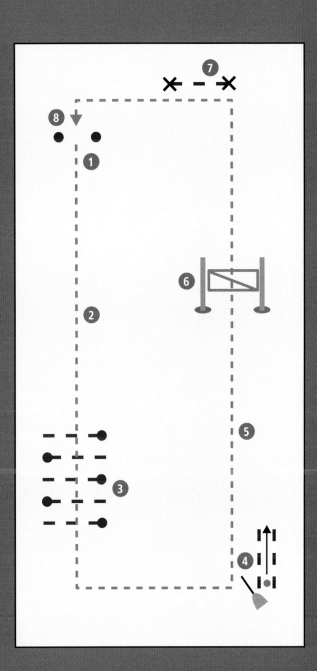

🖝 EXERCISE 21: TIMED AGILITY

Can be done at the trot to save time.

1. Enter at a walk, halt, and then proceed at the walk.

2. Weave between the cones.

3. Halt inside the pole chute, ring the bell, and then rein-back out of the chute.

4. Halt, and move the cup from the barrel on one side to the barrel on the other side.

5. Lead the horse through the U-shape pole chute.

6. Step over the poles.

7. Lead the horse into the pole square; halt, and then circle once around the cone.

8. Volte inside the cone lane.

9. Proceed into the high pole chute, and then halt.

10. Take the saddle pad from the pole to the left, place it on the horse, and then go around him and retrieve the pad from his other side to place it on the pole to the right.

11. Rein-back out of the chute, then proceed forward again.

12. Weave between the cones.

13. Halt and end the exercise.

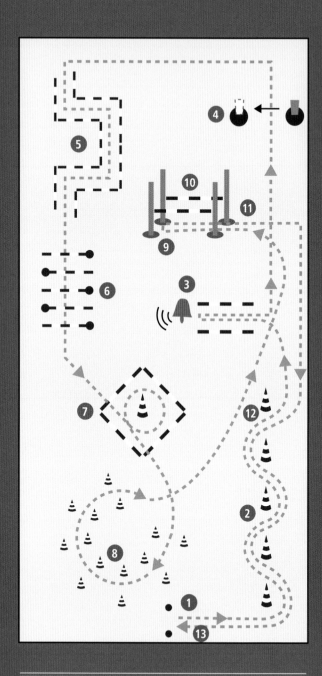

EQUIPMENT
— 20 cones
— 20 ground poles at least 10 feet (3 meters) long
— 4 ground poles at least 13 feet (4 meters) long
— 26 pole anchors
— 5 cavalletti
— 1 bell
— 1 saddle pad
— 4 jump standards
— 2 barrels and 1 cup

FIGURES AND DIMENSIONS
— Volte: inner group of cones 26 feet (8 meters) in circumference
— Weaving section: cones 29 feet (6 meters) apart
— Uneven row: poles about 2 feet (.6–.7 meters) apart

☞ EXERCISE 22: EXPERIENCED PONIES ONLY

1. Enter at the walk, halt, and then proceed at the walk.

2. Weave between the cones.

3. At this cone, transition to trot.

4. Turn right, transition back to walk.

5. Halt inside the pole chute, and then proceed at the walk.

6. Halt across the pole, and then proceed at the walk.

7. Track right; lead the horse through the double U-shape maze; track left.

8. Lead the horse across the tarp; when you reach the short side of the arena, turn right.

9. Transition to trot and trot on the first track.

10. Walk.

11. Cross under the pool noodle.

12. Weave between the cones.

13. Return to the starting point, halt, and end the exercise.

EQUIPMENT
— / cones
— 9 ground poles
— 18 pole anchors
— 1 pool noodle
— 2 jump standards
— 1 tarp

FIGURES AND DIMENSIONS
— Weaving section: cones 20 feet (6 meters) apart
— Double-U maze: poles 4 feet (1.2 meters) apart
— Pool noodle: about 5 feet (1.6 meters) high, depending on the height of the pony

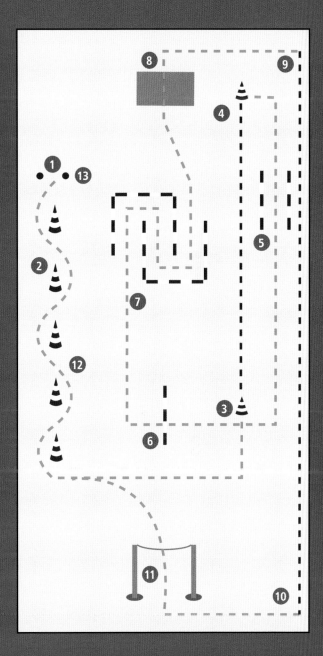

☞ EXERCISE 23: ACCURACY

1. Enter at a walk, halt at the starting point, and then proceed at the walk.

2. Pull the rattle sack from the square and bring it along.

3. Place the rattle sack in this square.

4. Take the lead rope in the left hand and direct the horse to walk a volte around you, 11 feet (3.5 meters) away from you. Then return to the normal leading position.

5. Lead the horse over the uneven row of ground poles.

6. Turnaround: walk through the pole chute into the square, turn around the pole in the center, and then exit again.

7. Trot.

8. Halt; proceed at the walk.

9. Halt; rein-back into cone chute.

10. Proceed at the walk, and return to the starting point; halt and end the exercise.

EQUIPMENT
— 9 cones
— 7 ground poles at least 10 feet (3 meters) long
— 4 ground poles at least 13 feet (4 meters) long
— 22 pole anchors
— 1 sturdy jump standard
— 1 rope at least 13 feet (4 meters) long
— 1 rattle sack"

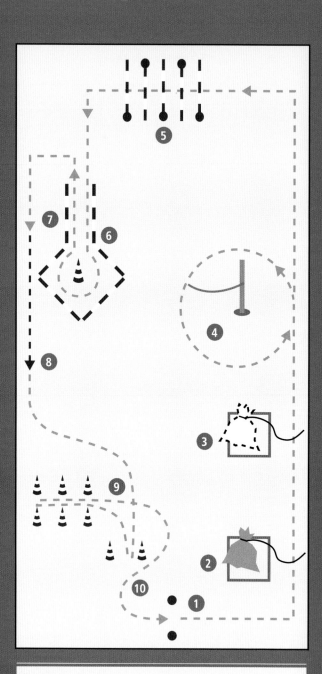

FIGURES AND DIMENSIONS
— Volte: 10 meters (32 feet) in diameter
— Uneven row: poles 5 feet (1.5 meters) apart
— Turnaround: entrance poles 5 feet (1.5 meters) apart and 10 feet (3 meters) long; square 13 feet (4 meters) across

LEAD LINES

Working with a lead line or groundwork line has multiple benefits. It's used to prepare young horses for traditional longeing, serves to control the horse at a distance, prepares the horse for mounted work, helps the horse become comfortable in his surroundings, makes it possible—with some practice—to work through agility and bombproofing obstacles at a distance, and can be used by experienced handlers to prepare the horse to load onto a trailer.

Initially, the setup consists of a rope halter or regular halter, and the lead line. The lead line should be 12–15 feet (3.8–4.8 meters) long, depending on the size of the horse.

The lead line can be up to 23 feet (7 meters) long to allow the handler to maintain a sufficiently safe distance from the horse, which is especially useful with young or unruly horses.

CHANGES OF SPEED AND GAIT

To ask a horse to walk on when leading at a distance, you position yourself in line with his barrel, facing him. The loops of the lead line are held by the hand leading the horse. You hold the line in a way that allows the pinky finger of that hand to point towards the horse's head. Then swing the end of the rope in a circling motion with the other hand, one time or several times, to move the horse away from you and onto a circle. In the moment when the horse walks off willingly, lessen the swinging motion of the rope. As the horse is walking away, the rope is let out until the horse is on a circle of the desired size. It's important to actively give with the rope. The horse should not have to pull on the rope to make the circle bigger. Always maintain a safe distance from his hindquarters, especially when applying forward driving aids.

The position of the handler depends on what she wants to achieve: to drive the horse forward, her position should be by his barrel but farther back, in line with his croup. To slow the horse down with halting aids, she should position herself farther to the front, in line with his shoulders or neck. To halt the horse, she should be in line with his head or even slightly ahead of him, to restrict his forward motion. While in a forward driving position, turn your body in the direction of travel, use voice cues, and, if necessary, swing the end of the lead line to clarify your intentions even further.

Should it be necessary to touch the horse, it's important to maintain a safe distance. To slow his tempo or transition into a slower gait, turn your body slightly against the direction of the horse's travel, and use voice cues in support of your aids. Through all transitions and into the halt, the horse should remain on the line of the circle.

Should the horse push to the inside of the circle, use the end of the lead line a circular motion toward the horse's shoulder to send him back out. If the horse doesn't respond to these cues, a touch with the leather end of the lead line can help clarify your request. When you're working at a distance, the lead line should hang somewhat slack, without touching the ground.

Leading the horse through the cones with a rope halter and lead line.

Working through the L-shape on long reins.

The lead line's own weight helps create a quiet, supple connection to the horse. The hand holding the line should be moving in a controlled and guiding manner. Even a slight swinging motion of the hand sends a signal through the lead line to the horse. In addition, the horse takes in the handler's body language and receives input that way. The handler's body language must convey where the horse is supposed to go, calmly and precisely.

— Walking circle lines of differing diameters

— Shifting the circle, walking an oval

— Switching between straight and bending lines

— Serpentines

— Changes of rein

Cones can be used to support the horse and to maintain his line of travel during bending drills.

WORKING WITH LONG REINS

Once you and the horse are both comfortable with all previous training and with a lead line where you are leading at a distance, it will be easy to develop this training further using long reins. The horse has learned to respond softly to cues and aids from his handler, and by now, he is used to his handler standing or walking at a distance from him, and to being sent in different directions from there. He should also be comfortable with the lead line touching him anywhere on his body.

At this point, a surcingle with training rings, a correctly fitted bridle, two long reins or lead lines that are about 16–20 feet (5–6 meters) long, and a short driving whip or bow-topped whip are part of the equipment. For younger horses, the long reins can be clipped to the halter's side rings, in combination with a bit.

For the first attempt, it's a good idea to have a helper who can hold the horse while you get into position behind the horse, and can help lead the horse until he has adjusted to this initially unfamiliar way to apply the aids. Stay about one horse-length (10 feet / 3 meters) behind the horse to maintain a safe distance.

The horse should follow the rein aids coming from the long reins, the driving aids coming from your voice, and possibly the supporting cues from the whip, at the desired speed and in the desired direction. Begin with the walk in different speeds: working walk, medium walk, and extended walk, as practiced previously during earlier groundwork training. If you are physically able to do so, you can also develop trot and canter with the long reins.

However, the main emphasis here is on building trust through work at the walk and on handling obstacles, in preparation for and in addition to riding or driving.

The left hand holds both reins. The left rein is held from the top down in the whole hand, and the right rein is kept between the middle and ring fingers. The whip is carried in the right hand. If the reins are held in both hands, it's more difficult to handle the whip, as you can no longer operate it independently from the reins.

Working on long reins, you and the horse can complete all sorts of different groundwork obstacles, and, with enough practice, will be able to go outside the arena. This kind of training is very similar to the skills necessary for riding. Rein and leg (whip) aids must be coordinated well to get optimal results that will enable the horse to cope with obstacles.

GROUNDWORK WITHOUT A ROPE AND LIBERTY WORK

Since you are working without a physical connection to the horse in the form of a lead rope, lead line, or reins, an enclosed area is a necessity. All groundwork exercises conducted with a lead rope can also be done without out a lead rope—even challenging tasks like halting from a trot, backing up, lateral movements, and more. The handler is near the horse, but without any direct physical interaction with the horse through ropes or reins. The horse's basic education must be solid, and the handler's body language must be clear and unambiguous for work without a rope to succeed. Once again, the rules of training apply: go from easy to hard, and from the familiar to the unfamiliar.

The exercises must logically build on one another, and must continue to be enjoyable for the horse. It's important to accommodate the horse's ability to focus. Pushing past his limits will lead to mistakes and failure.

During liberty work, the distance between handler and horse is determined by the size of the working area. The horse should be at a reasonable distance from his handler. Often, a longeing circle or round pen is used. The horse should move in all gaits in a composed manner, and should execute changes of direction, gait, and tempo by responding to his handler's body language and voice cues. Here, too, the horse's basic education and grasp of in-hand groundwork must be solid. The handler must be able to control her own

During liberty work, Caroline is close to the horse.

Trotting together with focus and attention.

movements and develop a good feel for the correct timing, the correct position, and the correct dosage in which to apply the aids. The goal is nearly invisible communication with the horse, which is only possible through trust, patience, and fairness.

☞ EXERCISE 24: WITH A LEAD LINE FROM A DISTANCE

1. Enter at the walk, leading with the right hand on the left side of the horse, and halt on the centerline.

2. Proceed at the walk onto a circle (volte), at least 10 feet (3 meters) from the horse, and then let the horse walk along the track.

3. Halt in the cone gate, and then proceed at the walk.

4. Volte around the cone at the trot: 8–10 meters (26–32 feet).

5. Transition to walk.

6. Lead the horse through the pole chute.

7. Turn toward the centerline and switch the side you're leading from.

8. Half a volte to the right.

9. On the first track, transition to trot and trot to the corner.

10. Lead the horse through a figure eight around the cones in the walk or the trot.

11. Weave between the cones (horse only; the handler should either stay at a distance, moving parallel to the horse, or switch the side she's leading from in front of the horse as he moves through the cones).

12. Return to the starting point, halt, and return to the horse's side; end the exercise.

EQUIPMENT
— 17 cones
— 2 ground poles
— 4 pole anchors

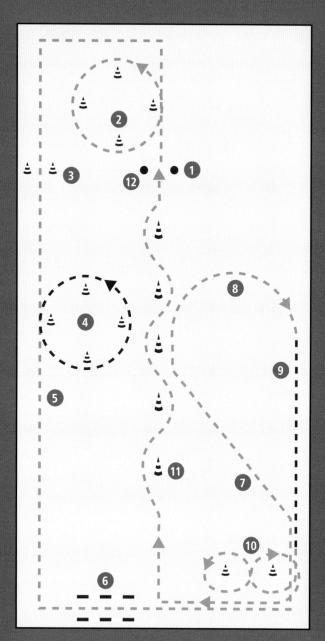

FIGURES AND DIMENSIONS
— Weaving section: cones 23 feet (7 meters) apart
— Figure eight: cones 19 feet (6 meters) apart and 10 feet (3 meters) from the track
— Cone gate: 4 feet (1.2 meters) wide

👉 EXERCISE 25: WITH LONG REINS

This is a sample exercise with long reins, executed in walk and trot.

1. Enter at the walk, with the handler about one horse-length, 10 feet (3 meters), behind the horse. Halt on the centerline, and then proceed at the walk.

2. Drive the horse through the cone gate.

3. Volte around the cones.

4. Drive the horse through a simple serpentine through the cone gates.

5. Drive the horse through the L-shape in the walk.

6. Halt, rein-back for 6 steps, halt again.

7. Proceed at the walk on the right rein.

8. Drive the horse through a figure eight around the cones in the walk.

9. Drive the horse through the L-shape.

10. Trot.

11. Return to the starting point, halt, and end the exercise.

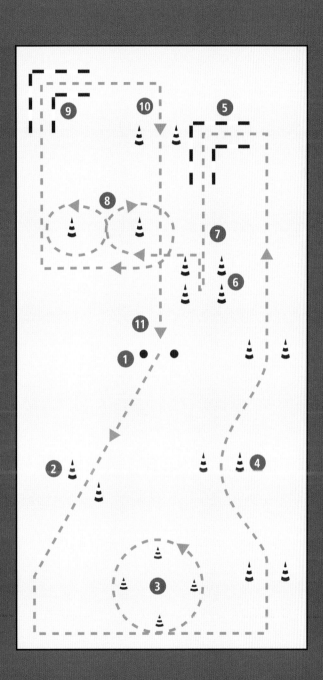

EQUIPMENT
— 26 cones
— 8 ground poles
— 16 pole anchors

FIGURES AND DIMENSIONS
— L-shape: poles 4–5 feet (1.2–1.5 meters) apart
— Figure eight: cones 19 feet (6 meters) apart
— Volte: cones positioned for a volte 10 meters (33 feet) in diameter

☞ EXERCISE 26: GROUNDWORK AT LIBERTY

This is a sample exercise at liberty, performed in the walk and trot.

1. Enter at a walk with a lead rope, leading with the right hand and walking on the left side of the horse. Halt on the centerline, take off the halter or unclip the lead rope, and then proceed at the walk.

2. Turn to the right.

3. Turn to the left.

4. Volte around the cones.

5. Trot.

6. Halt.

7. Rein-back for 6 steps.

8. Halt, switch the side you're leading from, and then walk on, across the short diagonal.

9. Volte.

10. Lead the horse through the narrow pole chute.

11. Figure eight; switch the side you're leading from as necessary during the walk.

12. Return to the starting point, halt, and end the exercise.

EQUIPMENT
— 14 cones
— 2 ground poles
— 4 pole anchors

FIGURES AND DIMENSIONS
— Figure eight: cones 19 feet (6 meters) apart
— Volte: cones positioned for a volte 8 meters (26 feet) in diameter

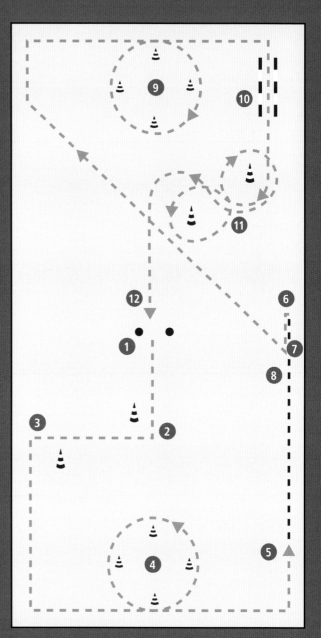